TERRY JONES'S WAR *on the* WAR ON TERROR

YOU MIGHT BE SURPRISED TO HEAR THIS...
BOOM
WHACK
WHAMMO
OOPS!
...BUT WE'RE NOT IN THE BUSINESS OF NATION BUILDING

Also by Terry Jones

Fiction

Fairy Tales - 1981

The Saga of Erik the Viking - 1983

Nicobobinus - 1985

Goblins of the Labyrinth - 1986

The Curse of the Vampire's Socks and Other Doggerel - 1988

Fantastic Stories - 1992

Lady Cottington's Pressed Fairy Book - 1994

Strange Stains and Mysterious Smells: Quentin Cottington's Journal of Faery Research - 1996

Douglas Adams' Starship Titanic - 1997

The Knight and the Squire - 1999

The Lady and the Squire - 2000

Fairy Tales and Fantastic Stories - 2003

Bedtime Stories - 2003

Nonfiction

Chaucer's Knight: The Portrait of a Medieval Mercenary -1980 (revised 1994)

Attacks Of Opinion - 1988

The Crusades - 1999 (with Alan Ereira)

Who Murdered Chaucer? - 2003 (with Robert Yeager, et al)

Medieval Lives - 2003 (with Alan Ereira)

with Michael Palin

Bert Fegg's Nasty Book For Boys and Girls - 1976

Dr. Fegg's Nasty Encyclopeadia (sic) Of All World Knowledge - 1984

Ripping Yarns - 1978

More Ripping Yarns - 1980

with the Pythons

Monty Python's Big Red Book - 1971

The Brand New Monty Python Bok - 1973

Monty Python & The Holy Grail - 1977

Monty Python's Life of Brian - 1979

Monty Python's The Meaning Of Life - 1983

A Pocketful of Python - 2002

The Pythons - 2004

TERRY JONES'S WAR
on the
WAR ON TERROR

Terry Jones

Illustrations by Steve Bell

NATION BOOKS
NEW YORK

TERRY JONES'S WAR ON THE WAR ON TERROR

Published by
Nation Books
An Imprint of Avalon Publishing Group
245 West 17th St., 11th Floor
New York, NY 10011

AVALON
publishing group incorporated

Nation Books is a co-publishing venture of the Nation Institute and Avalon Publishing Group Incorporated.

Library of Congress Cataloging-in-Publication Data is available.

ISBN 1-56025-653-2

9 8 7 6 5 4 3 2 1

The articles in this book first appeared in *The Guardian* (London) and *The Observer* (London)

"The Grammar of the War on Terrorism" by Terry Jones, taken from *Voices for Peace*, published by Simon & Schuster UK Ltd. in association with War Child. Reprinted by permission of Simon & Schuster UK Ltd.

Book design by Maria Elias
Printed in Canada
Distributed by Publishers Group West

CONTENTS

INTRODUCTION

Here is the news: There isn't any. Well, not much that's worth paying attention to. Newspapers, television, and radio all dance to the tune that those in power choose to pipe. Look at the *Washington Post*'s apology for its pre-Iraq War coverage. "Administration assertions were on the front page. Things that challenged the administration were on A18 on Sunday or A24 on Monday," admitted the paper's Pentagon correspondent Thomas Ricks.

Look at the fact that we call it the "Iraq War." Where was the war? Doesn't a "war" involve two sides fighting against each other? The "Iraq War" was simply one country (with a few hangers-on) dropping a lot of bombs on another country after it had sent in teams of inspectors to make sure that the country it was bombing didn't have any weapons to fight back with. I can't think of any "war" in history that has been conducted on a more cowardly basis.

We only call it a "war" because that's what George Bush and Tony Blair call it. Actually, the only "war" happened once the country had been occupied and a quisling government compliant to the U.S. agenda had been installed. As a consequence, we now have two sides fighting each other in the proper way. It's a war. But do the newspapers, television, and radio call it a "war"? No, they call it "insurgency" and "terrorism" because that's what Mr. Bush and Mr. Blair like to say it is. "

Those Iraqis who objected to the Americans bombing them, torturing their husbands and wives and friends in prisons, and who are now refusing to be governed by a puppet regime installed by Washington are designated "rebels"and "terrorists." And the *Washington Post* calls them "rebels" and "terrorists" with the rest, even though those forming the resistance are actually acting within the law—according to the provisions of the United Nations—by defending their country against a foreign occupation that the secretary general of the United Nations has declared illegal.

Well, you see where I'm coming from.

This book brings together a number of articles I wrote for various British newspapers—the *Observer*, the *Guardian*, and the *Independent*—in the wake of 9/11.

They represent my reactions to the reactions of Bush, Cheney, Rumsfeld, Blair, and Co. to what happened in New York City on that bright September morning. I suppose I was driven to write them because, as far as I could see, these people, who hold our fates in their hands, responded at every single stage with actions that would achieve the exact opposite of their stated intentions.

For example, Mr. Bush announced that he intended to catch the perpetrators of the attack on the Twin Towers.

Now, I would have thought that to catch a criminal one needs to exercise things like speed, secrecy, and surprise.

Mr. Bush, however, proceeded to announce to the world where he was going to look for these perpetrators (Afghanistan), when he was going to do the looking (in so many weeks time), and what he was going to do (bomb them). I would have thought that any perpetrators would have made themselves scarce long before the U.S. planes reached Afghanistan, which, in the event, is clearly what Osama bin Laden did.

Then again, both President Bush and Mr. Blair announced that their main objective was to rid the world of terrorism. Now, ignoring the fact that this is a pretty ridiculous sort of thing to announce in the first place, the way they went about it was obviously destined to increase terrorism rather than reduce it. Did either Mr. Bush or Mr. Blair honestly think that killing thousands of innocent men, women, and children in Afghanistan and Iraq was going to reduce hostility around the world?

We now know that Tony Blair was actually warned by his own experts in the Foreign Office that the results of bombing Iraq would be to expose the UK to an increased risk of terrorism, but even at the time it was blindingly obvious to many of us who weren't experts that that would be the case. It was clear that by attacking another country that was of no conceivable threat to our own we would mark ourselves as a terrorist target. It's not rocket science. It's plain common sense.

It was sufficiently obvious for millions of people to take to the streets to protest against their governments' plans for war. Has any population ever protested so vocally against its government's policies of aggression in the history of the world? I doubt it.

So it was that I found myself intrigued. Were Bush and Co. taking these absurd actions because they were stupid? Or was it simply that their declared policy objectives were not quite what they would have us believe?

To find some sort of answer to this question it wasn't much use turning to the news as reported in the newspapers, television, or radio. Comment articles were sometimes helpful but, by and large, to find out the real stories I had to turn to the Internet.

It's a sad reflection that I gained more information from certain Web sites than I could have done from any amount of hours spent watching TV. Particularly useful sites were: *Znet* (www.zmag.org), *Tom Paine* (www.tompaine.com), *Le Monde Diplomatique* (www.mondediplo.com), and the *New Standard* (www.newstandardnews.net).

But there was one Web site above all others that helped me to understand the motives of President Bush, Dick Cheney, Donald Rumsfeld, and Co. This is a Web site that I recommend everyone to take a look at, because it spells out with clarity and simplicity what it is that the people behind George W. Bush wish to achieve in the world.

And we can be sure that it is a pretty accurate representation of the White House and Pentagon's objectives because it is written by the very people who now run and advise both institutions—including the U.S. Deputy Defense Secretary Paul Wolfowitz and Richard Perle, former chairman of the Defense Policy Board that advises the Pentagon.

The Web site is called: the Project for the New American Century. It can be found at www.newamericancentury.org, and since 1997 it has been busy publishing reports, essays, and letters outlining the policies of the neoconservatives behind George W. Bush.

Their stated aim is "to shape a new century favorable to American principles and interests." They propose to achieve this by aggressive, preemptive military action wherever they think fit. "The history of the twentieth century should have taught us that it is important to shape circumstances before crises emerge, and to meet threats before they become dire. The history of the past century should have taught us to embrace the cause of American leadership."

In other words, war and violence are okay so long as it's America doing it. They claim, with some reason, that America has the might and it should use it to promote its interests around the world, but—and here is the "big but"—it should do it *regardless of international law and order*. Indeed, for the philosophers of the Pentagon, "international law and order" is a ridiculous and outdated concept.

Richard Perle was especially outspoken in his contempt for the institution of the United Nations. He called the UN "the chatterbox on the Hudson." (He was apparently unaware of its actual location on the East River.) And, he went on to say that the invasion of Iraq would spell the death of the UN and a good thing, too! "What will die is the fantasy of the UN as the foundation of a new world order," he wrote in the *Guardian*. All that will be left will be "the intellectual wreckage of the liberal conceit of safety through international law administered by international institutions."

You can see where he's coming from. And he is voicing the prevalent attitude of those now strutting through the corridors of power in the U.S.

But the Web site of the Project for the New American Century is even more revealing about President Bush's agenda in Iraq. It records for posterity the fact that, even before 9/11, the invasion of Iraq was high on the neo-con agenda. It wasn't triggered by the attack on the Twin Towers, even though that is what the media keeps telling us.

In September 2000, two months before George W. Bush was (or was not) elected president, the Project for the New American Century published a report called *Rebuilding America's Defenses*. In this report, to which the current U.S. Deputy Defense Secretary Paul Wolfowitz was a signatory, the Project made it clear that attacking Saddam Hussein was high on the priority list and that his removal had less to do with ridding the world of a nasty dictator than with establishing a new U.S. base in the Middle East.

"The United States has for decades sought to play a more permanent role in Gulf regional security," they wrote in the report. "While the unresolved conflict with Iraq provides the immediate justification, *the need for a substantial American force presence in the Gulf transcends the issue of the regime of Saddam Hussein*" (my italics).

One can only praise the authors of the report for their candor. They could not have spelled it out more clearly: Getting rid of Saddam Hussein was a side issue. The real purpose of the invasion was to establish an American "force presence" in the Land of Oil. The events of 9/11 were not the trigger for the invasion of Iraq—they were the pretext.

The authors also spelled out their determination to increase the U.S. government's spending on the military, writing, "The program we advocate—one that would provide America with forces to meet the strategic demands of the world's sole superpower—requires budget levels to be increased to 3.5 to 3.8 percent of the GDP."

Now, this is a thoroughly understandable aim—particularly when you bear in mind the close links that so many members of the administration have to the arms industry. Dick Cheney, former CEO of Halliburton, for instance, made $20.2 million from selling its shares when he became vice president and still receives $1 million per annum as "deferred compensation." They must think he's a really nice man or something to be worth all that. It is, of course, unthinkable, that, as vice president, he could have been instrumental in ensuring that Halliburton benefited from the Iraq adventure to the tune of billions of dancing dollars.

Similarly, Richard Perle, while he was still chairman of the Defense Policy Board, was busy briefing investors on how to make money out of U.S. conflicts with North Korea and Iraq. Unfortunately for Mr. Perle, the conflict of interest was too obvious even for the Bush regime and he was forced to step down as chairman, but the whiff of scandal didn't stop him still remaining a member of the Board with the potential to pass on inside information to his clients.

It's hard to come by information like this from the newspapers and almost impossible from the television. It's certainly no good expecting the TV commentators and interviewers to question a man as close to the president as Richard Perle on his shady business practices. No single interviewer has tried to probe him in depth on the issue of his conflict of interest.

But the Web site of the Project for the New American Century reveals even more. Of course, the authors of *Rebuilding America's Defenses* realized that while all this increase in spending on war would be welcomed by those involved in the arms and reconstruction industries, it might not go down so well with the general public, who would have to see cuts in spending on police, firefighters, and emergency medical workers, along with assistance for the poorest families and foreign war veterans and so on and so forth.

The Project people acknowledge this problem handsomely in their report. They note that the only thing that could save them from a long and arduous campaign to divert public money from educating the young or housing the homeless to lining the pockets of the war profiteers would be a catastrophic attack on the United States. They write in the report that "the process of transformation . . . is likely to be a long one, absent some catastrophic and catalyzing event like a new Pearl Harbor."

In other words, the attack on the Twin Towers was just what the neo-cons needed. One doesn't have to believe that they instigated the attack or condoned it or even simply turned a blind eye to it. But the evidence is there in their own words that "some catastrophic and catalyzing event" was exactly what was required to trigger the increased spending on warfare that they aimed for.

I suppose you could just say, "Well, lucky them!" They weren't guilty of anything, except for wishful thinking, but it doesn't make one feel at all comfortable to know that what happened on 9/11 fits so snugly into the agenda of those who run the U.S. of A.

So, I hope you enjoy the little outbursts of indignation contained in this book. They were written as the events were happening, or shortly after, and share the ignorance of what would happen next with the politicians who were perpetrating the action.

—Terry Jones
September 26, 2004
London

WE WILL HUNT THE TURRRSTS IN EV'RA DARK CORNER OF THE EARTH....
©Steve Bell 2003- 1927. 22.5.03-

1.

THE GRAMMAR OF THE WAR ON TERRORISM

from *Voices for Peace*,
Anna Kiernan (Editor), Scribner, 2001

What really alarms me about President Bush's "War on Terrorism" is the grammar. How do you wage war on an abstract noun? It's rather like bombing "murder."

"We're going to bomb 'murder' wherever it lurks," announced President Bush. "We are going to seek out the murderers and the would-be murderers wherever they are hiding and we are going to bring them to justice. We are also going to bomb any government that harbors murderers and murderers-to-be."

The other thing that worries me about Bush's and Blair's "War on Terrorism" is: How will they know when they've won it?

With most wars you can say you've won when the other side is either all dead or surrenders. But how is "terrorism" going to surrender? It's well known, in philological circles, that it's very hard for abstract nouns to surrender. In fact, it's very hard for abstract nouns to do anything at all of their own volition, and hard for even trained philologists to negotiate with them. It's difficult to find their hideouts, useless to try and cut off their supplies or intercept their paths of communication, and it's downright impossible to try and make them give in. Abstract nouns simply aren't like that. I'm afraid the bitter semantic truth is, you can't win against these sort of words—unless, I suppose, you get them thrown out of the *Oxford English Dictionary*. That would show 'em.

A nearby professor of ontological semiotics (currently working on finding out what his title means) informs me that the Second World War was fought against an abstract noun: "Fascism"—remember? But I point out to him that that particular abstract noun was cunningly hiding behind the very real persona of Nazi Germany. In 1945, we simply had to defeat Nazi Germany to win. In President Bush's "War on Terrorism," there is no such solution in sight. He can say, "We will destroy terrorism. And make no mistake we shall win!" until the chickens come home to roost, but the statement is about as meaningful as saying, "We shall annihilate 'mockery'" or "We shall deride 'persiflage.'"

Actually, the very word "terrorism" seems to have

changed its meaning over recent years. Throughout history, terrorism has been a favorite tool of governments—one thinks, for example, of Edward III's *chevauchée* across Normandy in 1359 (or possibly one doesn't). But in its current usage, "terrorism" cannot be committed by a country. When the USA bombed the pharmaceutical factory in the Sudan on the mistaken advice from the CIA that it was a chemical weapons factory, *that* was not an act of terrorism. It was pretty stupid. The resulting shortage of medicines probably killed thousands of people, but it was not an "act of terrorism" within the current meaning of the word, because the USA government did it officially. *And* they apologized for it. That's very important. No self-respecting terrorist ever apologizes. It's one of the few things that distinguishes legitimate governments from terrorists.

So, it was really difficult for President Bush to know whom to bomb after the World Trade Center outrage. If a country like Bermuda or New Zealand had done it then it would have been simple—he could have bombed the Bahamas and Australia. It must have been really irritating that the people who perpetrated such a horrendous catastrophe were not a nation. What's more, terrorists—unlike a country—won't keep still in one place so you can bomb them. Terrorists have this annoying habit of moving around and sometimes of even leaving the country. It's all very un-American (apart from the training, that is).

On top of all this, you really have no idea who the terrorists are. At least I assume the CIA and the FBI had no idea who the WTC terrorists were—otherwise, they'd have stopped them getting on the planes in the first place. It's in the very nature of terrorists not to be known until they've committed their particular act of terrorism. Otherwise, they're just plain old Tim McVeigh who lives next door, or that nice Mr. Atta who's taking flying lessons.

Well, you may say, there's that not-so-nice (although rather good at propaganda) Osama bin Laden—we know he's committed acts of terrorism and intends to do so again. Fine. At least we know one terrorist. But kill him and you still haven't killed terrorism. In fact, you haven't even begun to kill terrorism. That's the trouble with declaring war on terrorism. Being an abstract noun it cannot be defined by individuals or organizations.

Mr. Bush and Mr. Blair must be the first heads of state to lead their countries into a war in which they don't know who the enemy is.

So, let's forget the abstract noun. Let's rename President Bush's war for him, let's call it the "War on Terrorists"—that sounds a bit more concrete. But, actually, the semantics get even more obscure. What exactly does President Bush mean by "terrorists"? He hasn't actually defined the term for us, so we'll have to try and work out what he means from his actions.

Judging from President Bush's actions, the terrorists who instigated the attack on the World Trade Center all live together in camps in Afghanistan. There, apparently, they've all stuck together, after their successful mission, hanging around in these "camps" so that we can go and bomb the hell out of them. Presumably, they spend the evenings playing the guitar and eating their chow around the campfire. In these "camps," the terrorists also engage in "training" and stockpiling weapons, which we can obliterate with our cluster bombs and uranium-tipped missiles. Nobody seems to have told President Bush that the horrors of September were perpetrated with nothing more that a couple of dozen box cutters. I suppose the U.S. could bomb all the stockpiles of box cutters in the world, but I have a sneaking feeling it's still not going to eradicate any terrorists.

Besides, I thought the terrorists who crashed those planes into the World Trade Center were living in Florida and New Jersey. I thought the Al Qaeda network was operating in sixty-four countries, including the U.S. and many European countries that even President Bush might prefer not to bomb. But no, President Bush, the U.S. Congress, Prime Minister Blair, and pretty well the entire House of Commons are convinced that terrorists live in Afghanistan and can be bombed from a safe distance. What we are witnessing is clearly yet another example of a word changing its meaning.

It's often said that "in War the first casualty is grammar." President Bush's "War on Terrorism" is no exception. Statements no longer mean what they used to mean. For example, people keep saying to me: "We've got to carry on as normal." What are they talking about? The World Trade Center has been destroyed with the loss of thousands of lives and the U.S. and the UK are currently bombing Afghanistan. That doesn't sound like a definition of "normal" to me. Why should we pretend that it is?

And what is meant by: "We mustn't give in to the terrorists"? We gave in to the terrorists the moment the first bombs fell on Afghanistan, and the instigators of September 11 must have been popping the corks on their nonalcoholic champagne (I speak metaphorically, of course). They have successfully provoked the U.S. into attacking yet another poor country it didn't previously know much about, thereby creating genuine revulsion throughout the Arab world and ensuring that Islam is destabilized and that that support swings in favor of the Islamic fundamentalists.

Words have become devalued, some have changed their meaning, and the philologists can only shake their heads and wonder whether it isn't all just a huge grammatical mess.

2.

OSAMA LOOKS HAGGARD

December 28, 2001

Osama bin Laden is looking "haggard." A videotape broadcast on al-Jazeera TV showed the Most Wanted Man In The Known World looking *haggard*. And, in case we didn't notice how *haggard* he was actually looking, the Western media have been pounding us with the word ever since the pictures were released.

So, I would like to congratulate President Bush and Mr. Blair on the first concrete evidence that their "War on Terrorism" is finally achieving some of its policy objectives.

Of course, they've done terribly well in bringing chaos to Afghanistan, but I don't remember that as being one of the policy objectives. When those planes smashed into the Twin Towers with the loss of three and a half thousand innocent American lives, I don't think anybody's first reaction was: "Well, the sooner we get the Mujahideen and the warlords to take over Kabul the better!" No, as I remember, President Bush laid out his policy objectives of his "War on Terrorism" in measured terms: "We must catch the evil perpetrators of this cowardly act and bring them to justice."

Of course, bringing to justice the people who actually perpetrated the dreadful crime was out of the question since they were already dead. They'd killed themselves in a typically cowardly fashion. So, as I remember it, President Bush pretty quickly said he would get whoever egged them on to do it and then he would make *them* pay for it.

Well, many months later who has paid for it? The U.S. taxpayers have stumped up billions of dollars. They've paid for it. So have the British taxpayers, for some reason that hasn't yet been explained to us. Uncounted thousands of innocent Afghan citizens have paid for it, too—with their lives. I say "uncounted" because nobody in the West seems to have been particularly interested in counting them. It's pretty certain more innocent people have died and are still dying in the bombing of Afghanistan than on September 11, but the *New York Times* doesn't run daily biographies of them so they don't count.

Oh, I nearly forgot—we've all paid a considerable

amount in terms of those precious civil liberties and freedoms that make our way of life in the Free World so much better than everyone else's. Bit of a conundrum that.

We are all also paying a huge price, all the time, every day, in terms of our daily anxiety quota. We don't fly in planes or, if we do, we do so in fear and dread. All the time we are fearful of some nameless retribution being visited on us. And it's no good Tony Blair saying this is all the terrorists' fault. Of course it is, but then if we hadn't joined the Americans in bombing Afghanistan we wouldn't be running around so scared.

So, the objectives of the "War on Terrorism" were to catch the perpetrators of September 11, bring them to justice, and make the world a safer place.

Well, so far the score—on all three objectives—has been nil. We're all jumping around scared shitless that something similar is going to happen at any moment. No perpetrators have been caught. No perpetrators have been brought to justice.

Mark you, this last bit is not really surprising. Just think: If the police were setting out to catch a particularly clever and evil murderer, would they go around with loudspeakers announcing where they were going to look for him, pinpoint the areas they intended to search, and give him a count of hundred to get away? That's what you do if you're playing hide-and-seek, not if you want to catch a criminal. I imagine the police would have gone to work covertly and tried to find out where he was without his even knowing they were looking for him. Of course, I realize that's not a very American way of going about things.

However, as I say, the "War on Terrorism" is finally achieving its policy objectives. Osama bin Laden is looking *haggard*. We may not have caught Osama bin Laden or brought him to justice, but, at the cost of thousands of innocent Afghani lives, billions of dollars of U.S. citizens' money, and the civil liberties of the Free World, we have got him looking *haggard*.

It's a sensational and groundbreaking moment that justifies all the news coverage it's been getting. If Osama bin Laden is looking haggard, that means he's scared—or tired, or eaten something that disagrees with him—but at least it means he's not enjoying himself like he was in his last video. It is a considerable triumph for the U.S. forces, for the brave bomber pilots who release their bombs from such considerable and dangerous heights above the ground and, of course, for Tony Blair, who has so fearlessly led his entire nation into the position of being terrorist targets for no good reason that any of us can think of.

So, keep up the good work, President Bush and Mr. Blair, let's see if we can continue in this vein and perhaps—at the cost of only another few billion dollars, a lot more innocent lives, many more civil rights, and the stability of the Middle East, India, and Pakistan, and, perhaps, a Third World War—we might even be able to make Osama bin Laden frown or at least take the smile off his face.

3.

A BAG OVER THE HEAD IS WORTH TWO FOR GEORGE BUSH

January 3, 2002

I was thrilled to see a photo in the *New York Times* this week showing U.S. troops guarding prisoners suspected of belonging to Al Qaeda in Shibarghan, Afghanistan.

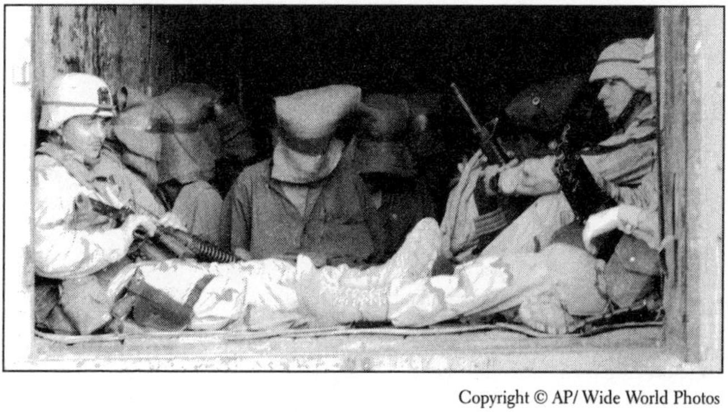

The story that accompanied the picture, described how soldiers from the 101st Airborne Division had been ordered to relieve the U.S. Marine Corps in southern Afghanistan, paving the way for a long-term military presence in the country.

The photo also appeared in *The Times* here, but neither newspaper mentioned the part of the photo that got me so excited as President of The Humane Society for Putting Bags over Suspects' Heads. The photograph clearly showed that the prisoners suspected of belonging to Al Qaeda had their arms pinioned behind them and had bags over their heads, secured with metallic tape.

We in HSPBOSH have been trying for years to get more armies to put bags over the heads of anyone they suspect of anything.

For one thing, the placing of a bag over the heads of suspects protects those of us who are not involved from unpleasant feelings of sympathy for the prisoners. There is nothing more offensive to ordinary, law-abiding newspaper readers than seeing rows of sorry-looking peasants being herded into the backs of cattle trucks by our boys in the army. The prisoners often looked frightened, dejected, and hungry, and how can anyone eat a decent full breakfast over photos like that?

Once a bag has been placed firmly over their heads, however, it is impossible to feel anything much for them.

They cease to be human beings and, as such, make no unreasonable call upon our emotions.

The placing of bags over the suspects' heads, also has another highly desirable effect. It instantly makes them all look guilty. One cannot see a man with a bag over his head without feeling that he must have deserved it, and that anything he has got coming to him is only what he ought to expect.

The same probably goes for the person with the bag over his head. I've never had it done to me personally, you understand, but I believe the effect is very disorientating. A prisoner with the bag over his head ceases to feel human as well as look it, and the deprivation of sight and smell and balance encourages him to expect the worst.

And this, of course, brings us to the economic argument for putting heads in bags. Once a suspect has been bound, had the bag placed over his head, and been driven around in the back of a cattle truck for a bit, he'll usually confess to anything. This saves a lot of time, effort and—most importantly—money in trying to sort out terrorists from ordinary blokes whom the army has rounded up because they had unpleasant beards and bad haircuts.

This is one of the reasons why the British government was so keen on putting bags over the heads of IRA suspects in the early '70s. It was economically very effective. Of course, those spoilsports at the European Court of Human

Rights put a wrench in the works in 1978 when they outlawed the technique, claiming that it "amounted to a practice of inhuman and degrading treatment." In other words, they said it was a form of torture.

Luckily, the U.S. is not bound by any soft-centered decisions of the European Court of Human Rights.

In fact, the U.S. also needn't take any notice of the United Nations Convention Against Torture either, because it was one of the few countries that had the sense not to sign the agreement in 1985. Argentina, Belgium, Bolivia, Costa Rica, Denmark, Dominican Republic, Finland, France, Greece, Iceland, Italy, Netherlands, Norway, Portugal, Senegal, Spain, Sweden, Switzerland, and Uruguay made the mistake of signing it, and subsequently Venezuela, Luxembourg, Panama, Austria, and even the UK and Afghanistan joined in, but America didn't.

Lucky for them. Now we can see how it's paying off. The U.S. Army can put bags over the heads of whoever they like.

But what really excited us at HSPBOSH was the fact that the editors of both the *New York Times* and *The Times* could publish a photograph of Afghanistani suspects with bags over their heads without making any comment at all. Clearly they assume that in the current world situation we all feel perfectly comfortable with the idea of putting bags over the heads of anyone we suspect we won't like.

Let's hope this means that the British and American public are finally ready to accept the fact that the only faces that matter are British and American faces. Those are the only "people" who count now and—to be quite honest—the rest of the world might as well go around with bags over their heads. Which is great news for all of us here at HSPBOSH.

THINK OF A NUMBER OF TERRSTS; MULTIPLY IT BY THREE...
...ADD ON THE TOADAL POPULATION OF ABROAD; CONVERT IT INTO DOLLARS...
©Steve Bell 2002 - 31.1.02 - 1711.

4.

THE STATE OF THE UNION ADDRESS:

A HOLLYWOOD SCRIPT READER'S REPORT

February 2, 2002

The State of the Union Address by George W. Bush shows blockbuster potential but may need some revision before it should be considered for production.

The State of the Union Address touches on themes that have proved popular with movie-going audiences over recent years. There is clearly a public appetite for stories in which the Forces of Good confront and eventually defeat the Forces of Evil in armed conflict. One calls to mind *Black Hawk Down* or *Band of Brothers*. The underlying concept of an all-powerful Force for Good, momentarily disadvantaged in the continual struggle with the Forces of Evil, but which triumphs in the end has a universal appeal—*Superman, Rambo, Spiderman, Batman*, etc.

The State of the Union Address confronts these serious issues with some success. "Evil is real," says the hero at one point, "and it must be opposed." These are sentiments that every cinema audience can get behind.

The script depicts the evil in question with admirable economy and simplicity: "Rarely has the world faced a choice more clear or consequential," the hero tells his admirers. "Our enemies send other people's children on missions of suicide and murder. They embrace tyranny and death as a cause and a creed."

This is Hollywood storytelling at its best. No need to ask any more about these evil enemies—they "send other people's children on suicide missions!" Zap! Bam! No decent action movie can afford to overcomplicate the story by delving into the motivation of the antagonists. How the situation has arisen in which the Forces of Evil can so manipulate "other people's children" is simply not relevant to the genre of the true action movie—especially a war movie.

If one is to allow maximum screen time for images of the Good Guys bombing the shit out of the Bad Guys and shooting them up in all the interesting and novel ways that

Ridley Scott can dream up, then it's best to keep the issues clear and simple.

Of course, it is advisable to sketch in a historical context for the Good Guys and this *The State of the Union Address* does with due emotional impact: "We stand for a different choice, made long ago, on the day of our founding . . ." One can already hear the John Williams score in the background. "We affirm it again today. We choose freedom and the dignity of every life. Steadfast in our purpose, we now press on. We have known freedom's price. We have shown freedom's power. And in this great conflict, my fellow Americans, we will see freedom's victory."

It's stirring stuff and should get cinema audiences cheering in their seats. However, there are some problems.

The dangers of limiting the antagonist's role to a single villain has recently been demonstrated by the CNN series *The War in Afghanistan*. In this, the original objective of finding and bringing to justice the archvillain, Osama bin Laden, had to be abandoned by the end of the series and the destruction of the Afghan capital Kabul substituted as a suitable climax.

The State of the Union Address ingeniously avoids this problem by postulating an "axis of evil" consisting of not one but several "outlaw states:" Iran, Iraq, and North Korea. It then multiplies the possibilities for violent conflict by supposing that the entire world is infiltrated by tens of thousands of potential terrorists, trained by Al Qaeda in Afghanistan since 1966, which "are now spread throughout the world like ticking time bombs set to go off without warning."

Clearly, there is enough potential violent conflict here for not just one movie but for a whole series of movies—enough, indeed, to keep any number of presidents in power for the forseeable future.

The downside to this, however, is the size of the budget required by this sort of action movie. It's been estimated that *The War in Afghanistan* has been costing over $30 million a day—a billion dollars a month. That's a lot to recoup in cinema seats. Even with full domestic and foreign sales, video rights, product placement, and merchandising, it's an expensive project.

George W. Bush Productions Inc. has just announced plans to increase yearly spending on its Pentagon War Films subsidiary by $120 billion over the next five years to $451 billion in 2007. Spending on props and catering alone (weapons and supplies) would swell from $61 billion a year to $99 billion a year.

Even with Tom Hanks, Tom Cruise, and Brad Pitt in the main roles, its hard to see how this sort of financing can recoup in the short term. And yet, as the hero of *The State of the Union Address* himself puts it: "America is no longer protected by vast oceans. We are protected from attack only by vigorous action abroad, and increased vigilance at home." And by "vigorous action abroad" he means, of course, bombing the guts out of any country that can be associated with the Forces of Evil, as defined earlier.

In short, we consider *The State of the Union Address* should make an excellent and popular movie. It neatly divides the World into "Goodies" and "Baddies" in a way that will appeal to audiences of even the most rudimentary intelligence. At the same time, it appeals to patriotic and nationalist instincts that should guarantee a sustained theatrical life.

The budget may seem to be excessively high, but against this one must bear in mind that the making of the movie will in itself help the economy. Money invested in war movies like *The State of the Union Address* creates jobs and, hopefully, can fuel an economic revival. As the president of George W. Bush Productions recently put it, there are all sorts of spin-offs and benefits for society as a whole: "Knowledge gained from bioterrorism research," for example, "will improve public health, stronger police and fire departments will mean safer neighborhoods, and stricter border enforcement will combat illegal drugs."

The aim of the war movie industry must be, in the long term, threefold, as President Bush says: "To win the war, to protect our people, and create jobs in America." We believe that *The State of the Union Address* could be turned into a movie that will achieve all these aims.

©Steve Bell 2001-1653-9-10-01-
EAT AIR BORNE DEATH
THE AGE OF IRONY IS DEAD!
...AND DON'T YOU FORGET IT!!
EAT NOURISHING SNACKS

5.

BOMBING FOR A SAFER WORLD

February 17, 2002

To prevent terrorism by dropping bombs on Iraq is such an obvious idea that I can't think why no one has thought of it before. It's so simple. If only the UK had done something similar in Northern Ireland, we wouldn't be in the mess we are in today.

The moment the IRA blew up the Horseguards' bandstand, the government should have declared its own "War on Terrorism." It should have immediately demanded that the Irish government hand over Gerry Adams. If they refused to do so—or quibbled about needing proof of his guilt—we could have told them that this was no time for prevarication and that they must hand over not only Adams but all IRA terrorists in the republic. If they tried to stall by claiming that it was hard to tell who were IRA terrorists and who weren't, because they don't go around wearing identity badges, we would have been free to send in the bombers.

It is well known that the best way of picking out terrorists is to fly thirty-thousand feet above the capital city of any state that harbors them and drop bombs—preferably cluster bombs. It is conceivable that the bombing of Dublin might have provoked some sort of protest, even if just from James Joyce fans, and there is at least some likelihood of increased anti-British sentiment in what remained of the city and, thus, a rise in the numbers of potential terrorists. But this, in itself, would have justified the tactic of bombing them in the first place. We would have nipped them in the bud, so to speak. I hope you follow the argument.

Having bombed Dublin and, perhaps, a few IRA training bogs in Tipperary, we could not have afforded to be complacent. We would have had to turn our attention to those states that had supported and funded the IRA terrorists through all these years. The main provider of funds was, of course, the USA, and this would have posed us with a bit of a problem. Where to bomb in America? It's a big place and it's by no means certain that a small country like the

UK could afford enough bombs to do the whole job. It's going to cost the U.S. billions to bomb Iraq and a lot of that is empty countryside. America, on the other hand, provides a bewildering number of targets.

Should we have bombed Washington, where the policies were formed? Or should we have concentrated on places where Irishmen are known to lurk, like New York, Boston, and Philadelphia? We could have bombed any police station and fire station in most major urban centers, secure in the knowledge that we would be taking out significant numbers of IRA sympathizers. On Saint Patrick's Day, we could have bombed Fifth Avenue and scored a bull's-eye.

In those American cities we couldn't afford to bomb, we could have rounded up American citizens with Irish names, put bags over their heads, and flown them in chains to Guernsey or Rockall, where we could have given them food packets marked "My Kind of Meal" and exposed them to the elements with a clear conscience.

The same goes for Australia. There are thousands of people in Sydney and Melbourne alone who have actively supported Irish republicanism by sending money and good wishes back to people in the republic, many of whom are known to be IRA members and sympathizers. A well-placed bomb or two Down Under could have taken out the ringleaders and left the world a safer place. Of course, it goes without saying that we would also have had to bomb various parts of London such as Camden Town, Lewisham, and bits of Hammersmith and we should certainly have had to obliterate, if not the whole of Liverpool, at least the Scotland Road area.

And that would be it really as far as exterminating the IRA and its supporters. Easy. The "War on Terrorism" provides a solution so uncomplicated, so straightforward, and so gloriously simple that it baffles me why it has taken a man with the brains of George W. Bush to think of it.

So, sock it to Iraq, George. Let's make the world a safer place.

©Steve Bell 2004-2122-17.8.04-
SEND IN THE US SUPREME COURT! THAT GUY'S BEEN ELECTED BY A MAJORITY VOTE!

6.

DUBYA'S GRAND VISION OF DEMOCRACY

April 14, 2002

After last weekend's shocking events in Venezuela, in which President Chavez was ousted in a free and fair democratic coup, only to be returned to office two days later on what seems to have been little more than the whim of the people, the leaders of the Free World have clearly been forced to reconsider the nature of democracy.

When asked whether the Bush administration now recognized President Chavez as Venezuela's legitimate president, a spokesman for President Bush conceded that although Mr. Chavez "was democratically elected" one had to bear in mind that "legitimacy is something that is conferred not just by a majority of the voters, however." [*sic*]

This clearly involves a fundamental reevaluation of what we understand by democracy, so I offer here some thoughts on what principles other than counting votes might confer legitimacy.

Since its ground-breaking experiments in vote counting in Florida two years ago, the United States of America has been universally recognized as the chief innovator in the field of democratic principles. It goes without saying, therefore, that one of the factors that confers legitimacy on any democracy must surely be approval by the United States.

It's no good if people blindly vote in any Tom, Dick, or Hugo if they're not acceptable to Washington. If this is true of Iraq, North Korea, Serbia, and the UK, it is doubly true of South America. And it's especially true of a country that happens to be the third largest supplier of oil to the U.S.

It's also no good imagining that landslide victories are any guide to legitimacy. Just because Chavez has twice been elected president by the largest margins in Venezuela's history, and just because his government has twice the number of elected representatives than its opponents have, doesn't mean it can go around passing any legislation it wants.

According to the "Florida Rules," the narrower the

margin of victory, the greater the legitimacy. In fact, if the victor actually has *fewer* people voting for him than the loser (almost half a million fewer in George Bush's case), then that is democracy's way of granting him carte blanche to do whatever he and his friends in the oil business want.

Another good measure of legitimacy, according to the "Florida Rules," is the number of interesting variations that can be introduced into the voting system. Florida led the way in the 2000 presidential elections with a confusing ballot design in Palm Beach County (a confusion that favored Bush by ten to one) and difficulties with the punch-card system in twenty-six out of the sixty-seven counties (that probably lost Gore something in the region of thirty thousand votes). Then there was also the question of setting up roadblocks and searches to prevent black voters getting to the ballot, and the novel expedient of simply not collecting some of the ballot boxes when they did.

The lack of this sort of experimentation in the Venezuelan elections must do a lot to harm the legitimacy of any so-called "president" in the eyes of the Bush administration. Especially in Mr. Bush's brother's eyes.

The truth is that democracy is not really served by having elections at all. That is why the Bush administration was so prompt to endorse the presidency of Pedro Carmona Estanga, the head of Venezuela's most important business association, who promised faithfully not to hold any elections for a year.

One thing that certainly does *not* confer legitimacy on any democratic government is passing legislation to benefit its own people. Chavez reformed the corrupt system that he inherited and established in its place "one of the most progressive constitutions in the world." He tried to redistribute land to benefit the poorest farmers, granted titles to the self-built homes of the barrios, increased the minimum wage, and enrolled over 1 million students in school who were previously excluded.

Nevertheless, according to the *New York Times*, "Mr. Chavez's record as president is terrible." He has failed to end corruption, put his supporters into government, and at one point during the riots, blocked press coverage. But, of course, what really destroys any claims to legitimacy he might have has been his meetings with Saddam Hussein, Muammar el-Qaddafi, and Fidel Castro.

In fact, rather than stifling the press and television, Mr. Chavez has been foolish enough to allow it total freedom, with the result that nine out of ten newspapers and four out of the five television stations are in the hands of vested interests who oppose his reforms.

These TV stations played a big part in organizing the demonstrations of April 12, by advertising the event every ten minutes. During the riots, they continually showed film of Chavez supporters firing rifles, while reporting that ten demonstrators had been killed and hundreds injured. All of which has been dutifully reported worldwide and—what's more—used against Chavez by the U.S. government.

However, an eyewitness reports that most of the dead were Chavez supporters killed by rooftop snipers belonging to the extreme Bandera Roja party. An assertion supported by the secretary of health for metropolitan Caracas, Pedro Aristimuño, who reported that of those who died "the most serious wounds were in the cranium and cheek. . . . They appeared to be shots from above."

If democracy is to conform to the high expectations placed on it by the president of the United States and his team, it will sooner or later have to accept the principles established in Florida. In the meantime, states like Venezuela may claim to be democracies, but the word will ring hollow in the ears of George Bush.

THE POSTMODERN RESOLUTE APPROACH
© Steve Bell 1999 ~ 1285 · 9 · 6 · 99 ~
YES
IT'S
PEACE
OR NOT

7.

THE AUDACIOUS COURAGE OF MR. BLAIR

September 22, 2002

I would like to pay a tribute to the courage of Tony Blair. During these dark days in the build up to war against Iraq it is reassuring to find ourselves with a leader who demonstrates such fearlessness in the face of tremendous odds.

Despite bitter opposition, Tony Blair has demonstrated that he will push ahead stalwartly with whatever the U.S. intends to do. Even though the majority of his fellow countrymen are against the war (despite last week's propaganda campaign in the media), Mr. Blair has shown not the slightest sign of wavering from his determination to do whatever Mr. Bush wants. It is true that he has regrettably had to cave in over the question of debating the issue in Parliament, but he has fearlessly shown his contempt for the process by not allowing a vote. Mr. Blair realizes that he needs all the nerve he can command to resist demands for democratic discussion, if Mr. Bush is to have any opportunity of dropping bombs on Iraq before the midterm elections.

I would like to say a special word about another side of Tony Blair's courage—his moral courage. Tony Blair has the guts to stand on platform after platform repeating the words of the president of the United States even though he must be well aware that in so doing he makes himself a laughingstock to the rest of the world. Tony Blair has the balls not to be influenced by the knowledge that people imagine he is the U.S. president's parrot and that his knee jerks only when George W. pulls the strings. It must take a very special kind of stamina to withstand that sort of daily humiliation. It is time we gave Mr. Blair credit for it.

Tony Blair's dedication to carrying out the policies of the White House proves time and again that he has the courage of their convictions. He is prepared to back Mr. Bush's arguments to the hilt even when they are palpably nonsensical. When Mr. Bush cites Saddam Hussein's contempt for UN Security Council resolutions as the justification for his own determination to do the same, Tony Blair urges the president's case for all the world, as if he couldn't see the ridiculousness of it. When Mr. Bush cites Iraq's failure to comply with UN Security Council resolutions as the reason for going to war, Mr. Blair backs him up, boldly ignoring the fact that Turkey and Israel have gotten away with ignoring UN resolutions for years.

It is this refusal to be intimidated by the illogicality of the U.S. position that perhaps displays Mr. Blair's courage at its best. He is Mr. Bush's faithful echo when the president demands that Saddam Hussein immediately cleanse Iraq of all terrorist organizations, even though he knows the UK never found a way of eradicating the IRA, and that, in any case, the terrorist organizations that perpetrated 9/11 were operating out of the U.S. and Germany.

Mr. Blair also refuses to be unnerved by the irony of Saddam's chemical weapons being anathematized by the nation that employed Agent Orange so liberally in Vietnam, where the ravages are still apparent. Mr. Blair is unafraid to support a "War on Terrorism" waged by the nation that has routinely used terrorism as a tool of foreign policy in Chile, Colombia, Nicaragua, and Cuba, to name but a few.

But my admiration for Mr. Blair's courage reaches new depths when I consider what he has had to wrestle with over the matter of the sanctions against Iraq. As a practicing Christian, he must need tremendous fortitude to bear the knowledge that his policies are the certain cause of death to so many Iraqi children. In 1996, the World Health Organization concluded that since the introduction of sanctions, the infant mortality rate for children under five had increased six times. In 1999, the Mortality Survey, supported by Unicef, reported that infant and child mortality in Iraq had doubled since the Gulf War.

In May 2000, a mission to Iraq sponsored by the United Nations Food and Agriculture Organization (FAO) found that in South and Central Iraq at least eight-hundred thousand children under five were suffering from chronic malnutrition.

Despite the fact that George W. Bush's father claimed that the United States had no quarrel with the Iraqi people, it is the Iraqi people whom he and his successors have determined to punish, and Tony Blair, to do him justice, has not flinched from following their lead.

The Gulf War witnessed one of history's heaviest bombing campaigns, a forty-three-day bomb-fest, largely by units of the U.S. Air Force, left something in the region of $170 billion-worth of damage. The subsequent enforcement of sanctions has meant that much of that damage has never been repaired, and it is the lack of safe water, housing, food, and medicine that is exacting the greatest toll among children and the elderly.

It is, therefore, very much to Tony Blair's credit that he

refuses to be intimidated by these realities. He has had the grit to stick by those U.S. policies that target the most vulnerable sections of Iraqi society, and he has courageously ignored the logic that sanctions aimed at a civilian population in order to oust a dictator who cares little for his people are pointless.

It is a bold and audacious stance that our leader has taken up and it is clear that nothing will move Mr. Blair from that posture—not democracy, common sense, compassion, nor shame.

DON'T YOU WORRY NONE...
...I WON'T LET NO EVILDOERS WHACK MY WOLFIE!!!

8.

GEORGE W. BUSH'S LINKS TO AL QAEDA—WE HAVE THE FACTS

October 17, 2002

I am in a position to tell you categorically that George W. Bush's links to Al Qaeda are no longer simply obvious but are now proved beyond a shadow of doubt.

Using the same painstaking techniques that have been used over the last few weeks to identify Saddam Hussein with Al Qaeda and, more recently, the Bali bombing, it is at last possible to see how the president of the United States has secretly been working as an Al Qaeda agent, while posing as the leader of the Free World.

Of course, as with Saddam Hussein, the links cannot be proven beyond a shadow of a doubt. But we cannot wait for proof, since both are amassing Weapons of Mass Destruction. (Please repeat as many times as possible.) It is these same Weapons of Mass Destruction that link them irrefutably to The Best-Known Terrorist Organization in the World.

Look at it like this: If Saddam were linked to The Best-Known Terrorist Organization in the World (as he undoubtedly is) and he did use these Weapons of Mass Destruction we would all look pretty silly, wouldn't we, if we hadn't bombed the Iraqi people first. Does that make sense?

Anyway, the possession of Weapons of Mass Destruction is so terrifying we can't afford to waste time splitting hairs about how close or not anyone's ties to Al Qaeda may be—the mere fact that someone has Weapons of Mass Destruction is enough.

We cannot stand idly by and wait for George W. Bush to strike first. The destruction may be on a devastating scale.

But, you may say, what on earth would George W. Bush have to gain from encouraging Al Qaeda—an organization sworn to the destruction of his own society? The answer is: no more and no less than Saddam Hussein. The secular state that Saddam has established in Iraq is precisely the sort of enervated, pusillanimous Islamic society that Osama bin Laden's strict Wahabis or Salafis (as they prefer to be called) want to annihilate. Actually, they probably wouldn't mind annihilating most other forms of Islamic state but that's another story.

But, you may say, George W. Bush and Osama bin Laden are bitter enemies. Exactly the same with Saddam Hussein. He and Osama are enemies from way back. They may be both nominally Sunni Muslims but to imagine them on the same side is a bit like imagining Ian Paisley and Gerry Adams having a bath together.

Weapons of Mass Destruction. (Sorry, I hadn't said that for a while.)

But enough of the facts.

It has been obvious for some time now, that George W. has been working tirelessly and quite openly to encourage and sustain the Al Qaeda network.

Take for a start the president's actions immediately after September 11. Al Qaeda's long-term aim in bombing the Twin Towers was, doubtless, to rally the forces of Islamic fundamentalism in a jihad or holy war against America. To do this, of course, they need to stoke the flames of resentment against America, convert moderate Muslims to the fundamentalist cause, and spread hatred of everything American over the entire Arab world—precisely the achievements of George W. Bush's policies since September 11.

If George W. Bush had wanted to destroy U.S.-Arab

relationships, turn a lot of moderate Muslims into fanatics and cause deep resentment not just in the Arab world but in Europe, he could have done no better than by bombing the people of Afghanistan who had absolutely no more to do with the terrible events in New York than did the people of Hamburg or Florida. The only sane motive one can attribute to his actions is that he is doing the work of Al Qaeda for them.

The bombing of Iraq will certainly augment and support this process beyond the wildest dreams of Al Qaeda.

Similarly, instead of declaring the terrorists of September 11 criminals and relying on his own secret services and on police forces 'round the world to catch the perpetrators, he declared a "War on Terrorism"—thereby elevating the terrorists to the status of a nation state and making Al Qaeda The Best-Known Terrorist Organization in the World. Weapons of Mass Destruction. (Sorry!)

Instead of acting with secrecy and patience in order to infiltrate the terrorist cells, he publicly warned them for two weeks exactly where he was going to look for them, what he was going to do when he found them (i.e., drop bombs from a great height), and when he was going to do it.

George W. Bush's actions were clearly not those of a man who wished to catch the perpetrators. As indeed he did not. Not a single one.

More than that! His policies since September 11 can

only be explained as the acts of someone working on behalf of the terrorist organization. Most of President Bush's foreign policy initiatives have clearly been designed to boost recruitment to Al Qaeda—rather than reduce it. President Bush has persuaded thousands of young Arabs that Al Qaeda is a glamorous and honorable institution on a par with the governments of most Western states, who now cringe in fear before the mighty name of Osama bin Laden, while, at the same time, dismantling their own civil liberties and safeguards.

The same scrupulous research that the president and his advisers have given to Saddam Hussein's links to Al Qaeda, has also ennabled George W. Bush to immediately assign the Bali bombing to the same organization, rather than to the local Philippine Islamic fundamentalist groups: Jemaah Islamiyah or Laskar Jihad.

By applying the same standards of in-depth investigation and conscientious regard for the truth, we are thus able to state, without a shadow of doubt, that George W. Bush is an Al Qaeda agent working for the destruction of the Western World as we know it.

I am sending a dossier of all the relevant material to Tony Blair.

9.

COULD TONY BLAIR LOOK AT THE INTERNET NOW, PLEASE?

February 27, 2003

It's heartwarming to hear Tony Blair's concern for the plight of the Iraqi people and how the only possible way to help them is to bomb them with everything the Americans have.

Mr. Blair's sudden sympathy for the Iraqis' political aspirations comes as a welcome relief after all these years of U.S.-UK-led sanctions, which have caused the deaths of over half a million Iraqi children, according to the UN.

But I'm a bit worried that Tony may be deluding himself that his friends in the White House share his altruistic ideals.

I'm sure Tony has been reading all the recent stuff about PNAC*—The Project for the New American Century—but has he looked at their Web site?

As everybody knows, the PNAC is a think tank founded in 1997 by the people who are now closest to President Bush—Dick Cheney, Donald Rumsfeld, Paul Wolfowitz, Jeb Bush, and so on. It's a pretty safe bet that what PNAC thinks is what George W. Bush thinks. PNAC represents the thinking of the men now in power in the United States.

PNAC's stated aims are: "to shape a new century favorable to American principles and interests," to achieve "a foreign policy that boldly and purposefully promotes American principles abroad," "to increase defense spending significantly," and to pursue "America's unique role in preserving and extending an international order friendly to our security, our prosperity, and our principles."

They don't split hairs at the PNAC. George W. Bush and his advisers' stated aim is to ensure that America and American interests dominate the entire world for the foreseeable future. And what's more they make no bones about the fact that they intend to achieve this without diplomacy—that's old hat. What PNAC intends to do is enforce the Pax Americana through military might.

*The Project for the New American Century can be found at www.newamericancentury.org.

Does Tony Blair know that?

Has Tony Blair read the PNAC report called "Rebuilding America's Defenses 2000"? It refers to the new technologies of warfare and goes on:

"Potential rivals such as China are anxious to exploit these transformational technologies broadly, while adversaries like Iran, Iraq, and North Korea are rushing to develop ballistic missiles and nuclear weapons *as a deterrent to American intervention in regions they seek to dominate.*"

So, when George Bush and his colleagues talk about Saddam Hussein posing a "threat" to America—they don't mean he's going to drop bombs on Washington. (How on earth could he without committing national suicide?)—what they mean is that he poses a threat to American military dominance in the Middle East.

Does Tony Blair know that's what they mean?

In fact, does Tony Blair know that President Bush's advisers regard Saddam Hussein as merely an excuse for military action in the area? The PNAC report of 2000 states: "The United States has for decades sought to play a more permanent role in Gulf regional security. While the unresolved conflict with Iraq provides the immediate justification, *the need for a substantial American force presence in the Gulf transcends the issue of the regime of Saddam Hussein.*"

So, Iraq is merely "the immediate justification" and

Saddam's regime is not so important as establishing American military might in the Gulf.

Does Tony Blair know that?

If he has read PNAC's report he knows that he is simply aiding U.S. right-wing militarism and extremist Republican plans for world domination. Surely, in such a case, he would not be prepared to expose the British people to the nightmare of permanent terrorist threats and attacks. Surely, for such a cause, he would not be prepared to set fire to the Middle East, to destabilize the entire world for the foreseeable future and—most importantly perhaps—to risk his own political neck by pursuing an evil and almost universally despised policy.

On the other hand, if Tony Blair has not read "Rebuilding America's Defenses 2000" or gone to the PNAC Web site to learn exactly what motivates Rumsfeld, Cheney, Perle, Wolfowitz, and so on, then why the hell hasn't he?

Go to your computer now, Mr. Blair. Look at the reality behind all this sanctimonious wringing of hands over the plight of the Iraqi people. Read what your American Republican friends are really intending. Please.

10.

I'M LOSING PATIENCE WITH MY NEIGHBORS, MR. BUSH

January 26, 2003

I'm really excited by George Bush's latest reason for bombing Iraq: He's running out of patience. And so am I!

For some time now I've been really pissed off with Mr. Johnson, who lives a couple of doors down the street. Well, him and Mr. Patel, who runs the health-food shop. They both give me queer looks, and I'm sure Mr. Johnson is planning something nasty for me, but so far I haven't been able to discover what. I've been 'round to his place a few times to see what he's up to, but he's got everything well hidden. That's how devious he is.

As for Mr. Patel, don't ask me how I know, I just know—from very good sources—that he is, in reality, a mass murderer. I have leafletted the street telling them that if we don't act first, he'll pick us off one by one.

Some of my neighbors say, if I've got proof, why don't I go to the police? But that's simply ridiculous. The police will say that they need evidence of a crime with which to charge my neighbors.

They'll come up with endless red tape and quibbling about the rights and wrongs of a preemptive strike and all the while Mr. Johnson will be finalizing his plans to do terrible things to me, while Mr. Patel will be secretly murdering people. Since I'm the only one on the street with a decent range of automatic firearms, I reckon it's up to me to keep the peace. But, until recently, that's been a little difficult. Now, however, George W. Bush has made it clear that all I need to do is run out of patience, and then I can wade in and do whatever I want!

And let's face it, Mr. Bush's carefully thought-out policy toward Iraq is the only way to bring about international peace and security. The one certain way to stop Muslim fundamentalist suicide bombers targeting the U.S. or the UK is to bomb a few Muslim countries that have never threatened us.

That's why I want to blow up Mr. Johnson's garage and kill his wife and children. Strike first! That'll teach him a lesson. Then he'll leave us in peace and stop peering at me in that totally unacceptable way.

Mr. Bush makes it clear that all he needs to know before bombing Iraq is that Saddam is a really nasty man and that he has Weapons of Mass Destruction—even if no one can find them. I'm certain I've just as much justification for killing Mr. Johnson's wife and children as Mr. Bush has for bombing Iraq.

Mr. Bush's long-term aim is to make the world a safer place by eliminating "rogue states" and "terrorism." It's such a clever long-term aim because how can you ever know when you've achieved it? How will Mr. Bush know when he's wiped out all terrorists? When every single terrorist is dead? But then a terrorist is only a terrorist once he's committed an act of terror. What about would-be terrorists? These are the ones you really want to eliminate, since most of the known terrorists, being suicide bombers, have already eliminated themselves.

Perhaps Mr. Bush needs to wipe out everyone who could possibly be a future terrorist? Maybe he can't be sure he's achieved his objective until every Muslim fundamentalist is dead? But then, some moderate Muslims might convert to fundamentalism. Maybe the only really safe thing to do would be for Mr. Bush to eliminate all Muslims?

It's the same on my street. Mr. Johnson and Mr. Patel

are just the tip of the iceberg. There are dozens of other people in the street who I don't like and who—quite frankly—look at me in odd ways. No one will be really safe until I've wiped them all out.

My wife says I might be going too far but I tell her I'm simply using the same logic as the president of the United States. That shuts her up.

Like President Bush, I've run out of patience, and if that's a good enough reason for the president, it's good enough for me. I'm going to give the whole street two weeks—no, ten days—to come out in the open and hand over all aliens and interplanetary hijackers, galactic outlaws, and interstellar terrorist masterminds, and, if they don't hand them over nicely and say "Thank you," I'm going to bomb the entire street to kingdom come.

It's just as sane as what George W. Bush is proposing—and, in contrast to what he's intending, my policy will destroy only one street.

11.

HOW TO BOMB AND SAVE MONEY

January 30, 2003

There is a debate going on in the White House as to whether or not to use funds from the Iraqi oil fields to help pay for the American invasion of Iraq. I don't know what there is to debate. It's a brilliant idea.

Now, I know there are bound to be a few spoilsports who say that the oil from the Iraqi oil fields belongs to the Iraqi people and that the U.S. has no right to pinch any of it. But, let's face it, the Iraqi people are going to have the privilege of being bombed by the most modern, best-equipped, and most expensive army in the whole world; it's only right and proper that they should pay for it.

But how much? That's the question.

According to the Congressional Budget Office, the initial deployment of troops will cost the American taxpayer between $9 to $13 billion. Conducting the war is estimated at $6 to $9 billion per month and getting the forces home at $5 to $7 billion. While the occupation of Iraq itself will cost between $1 to $4 billion a month.

So, what would be a fair way of estimating how much the Iraqis pay for all this? I suggest they should pay by results.

A secret UN report reckons the American-British attack on Iraq is likely to produce five-hundred thousand casualties—that is, half a million Iraqi citizens will "require medical treatment to a greater or lesser degree as a result of direct or indirect injuries," according to the World Health Organization. Approximately 3.03 million Iraqis will suffer from malnutrition. Perhaps even more since sixteen million currently rely on a "food basket" provided by the Iraqi government. So, let's say ten million will suffer from starvation. Two million will be displaced, and perhaps another one million will become refugees. About 3.6 million will need "emergency shelter."

As my contribution to the war effort, I would like to suggest the following tariff as a way of containing the unimaginable costs of this great Anglo-American humanitarian undertaking.

For every adult Iraqi killed, I suggest the Iraqis should pay the Americans $1,000. For every Iraqi child under twelve, the Iraqis should pay the Americans on the following scale: Five hundred dollars for those children killed outright and $400 for those children who die within a month as a result of injuries sustained.

For every infant under the age of three, the Iraqis should pay the U.S. $12.50. For newborn babies blown to bits or crushed under collapsing hospital buildings: $1. For any child killed or mutilated as a result of the military action but who was going to die anyway from malnutrition as a result of the sanctions, the U.S. Treasury should be paid a token fee of 25¢ only.

For the wounded, I would suggest $15 for every limb severed with a premium of $10 for the loss of the right arm and an extra $20 if they should lose both. If a whole family is wiped out, the Iraqi government should pay the U.S. $2,000. Any family made homeless as a result of the chaos created by Allied action should pay the Americans $500. Individuals made homeless should be charged a flat fee of $100.

Those deprived of drinking water as a result of the bombing should pay a special charge of $50 regardless of whether or not they have already paid for any injuries sustained. Those who starve to death should be paid for on a flat rate of $100.

Those who contract cholera or typhoid as a result of

the anticipated disruption to the sewage system and drinking water supplies should pay the U.S. government $30 and cover the costs of any medical aid they might need, whether or not they receive it.

On this basis, if we are lucky enough to chalk up two-hundred thousand Iraqi civilians killed outright that would provide $2 billion. Ten million suffering from starvation would provide the U.S. Treasury with around $1 billion and five million homeless would put another $5 billion into the government's nest egg.

Of course, this would only pay for one month's occupation, and the rest would have to be found amongst American taxpayers. So, perhaps the fairer way would be for the above charges to be levied on a monthly basis.

I hope President Bush will take this proposal seriously, and that I have contributed to the well-being of our two great countries and have helped Mr. Bush in his ambition to further the principles of humanity and democracy by bombing innocent people who have never done him the slightest harm.

©Steve Bell 2001 - 1660 - 19 - 10 - 01 -
I ASK YOU - WHAT SORT OF MANIAC LEAVES WEAPONS-GRADE ANTHRAX LYIN' AROUND?

12.

COLIN POWELL'S EXPLODING ENGLISH

February 23, 2003

It was interesting to hear Colin Powell accuse France and Germany of cowardice in not wanting to go to war. Or, as he put more succinctly, France and Germany "are afraid of upholding their responsibility to impose the will of the international community." Powell's speech brings up one of the most outrageous but least examined aspects of this whole war on Iraq business. I am speaking about the appalling collateral damage already being inflicted on the English language.

Perhaps the worst impact is on our vocabulary. "Cowardice," according to Colin Powell, is the refusal to injure thousands of innocent civilians living in Baghdad in order to promote U.S. oil interests in the Middle East. The corollary is that "bravery" must be the ability to order the deaths of one-hundred thousand Iraqis without wincing or bringing up your Caesar salad.

I suppose Tony Blair is "brave" because he is willing to expose the people who voted for him to the threat of terrorist reprisals in return for getting a red carpet whenever he visits the White House, while Chirac is a "coward" for standing up to the bigoted bullying of the extremist right-wing Republican warmongers who currently run the United States.

In the same vein, well-fed young men sitting in millions of dollars' worth of military hardware and dropping bombs from thirty-thousand feet on impoverished people who have already had all their arms taken away are exemplars of "bravery." "Cowardliness," according to George W. Bush, is hijacking an aircraft and deliberately piloting it into a large building. There are plenty of things you could call that, but not "cowardly." Yet, when Bill Maher pointed this out on his TV show, *Politically Incorrect*, he was anathematized and the sponsors threatened to withdraw funding from the show.

Something weird is going on when not only do the politicians deliberately change the meanings of words, but also society is outraged when someone points out the correct usage.

Then there's "the international community." Clearly, Colin Powell cannot be talking of the millions who took to the streets last Saturday. The "international community" he's talking about must be those politicians who get together behind closed doors to decide how best to stay in power and enrich their supporters by maiming, mutilating, and killing a lot of foreigners in funny clothes whom they'll never see. And, while we're at it, what about that word "war." My dictionary defines a "war" as "open, armed conflict between two parties, nations, or states." Dropping bombs from a safe height on an already hard-pressed people, whose infrastructure is in chaos from years of sanctions and who live under an oppressive regime, isn't a "war." It's a turkey shoot.

But then the violence being done to the English language is probably the price we have to pay for cheap petrol.

Language is supposed to make ideas clearer so that we can understand them. But when politicians such as Colin Powell, George W. Bush, and Tony Blair get hold of language, their aim is usually the opposite. That's how they persuade us to take ludicrous concepts seriously. Like the whole idea of a "War on Terrorism." You can wage war against another country, or on a national group within your own country, but you can't wage war on an abstract noun. How do you know when you've won? When you've got it removed from the *Oxford English Dictionary*?

When men in power propose doing something that is shameful, wrong, and destructive, the first casualty is the English language. It would matter less if it were the only casualty. But if they carry on perverting our vocabulary and twisting our grammar, the result will spell death for many human beings who are now alive.

13.

SHAME ON BLAIR

February 23, 2003

Shame on Blair:

A war involves two sides threatening each other and attacking each other. What George Bush is proposing is to drop bombs on Baghdad from a safe height. How on earth is killing thousands of innocent civilians supposed to help them escape from their oppressor? How is bombing the cradle of civilization supposed to advance civilized values? The proposed policy does the very reverse of everything it claims to be trying to achieve. It will not make the world a safer place and it will not reduce the threat of terrorism.

On the contrary, the Middle East will become destabilized and we can probably look forward to twenty years of bloodshed in the area and escalating violence around the world.

As for terrorism, of course the policy has already increased the threat to unimaginable levels. Blair has willingly put the UK in the front line of terrorist attacks as the price to pay for the enthusiastic hospitality he enjoys in the White House.

It's stark-staring obvious. I cannot even believe we are here in 2003 discussing whether or not to drop bombs on a country that has never threatened us.

I refuse to have thousands of innocent Iraqis maimed, killed, and mutilated in my name. Blair should be ashamed of himself and of his reckless, bloodthirsty, and hypocritical policy.

14.

WHY SHOULDN'T BUSH KILL?

March 7, 2003

Mr. Bush is right, Saddam Hussein is a nasty man and nobody I know has the least objection to Mr. Bush killing him. It's just the way he proposes doing it that worries me. Dropping three-thousand bombs in forty-eight hours on Baghdad is going to kill a lot of other people who, as far as I am aware, are not nasty at all.

That's the bit of the "moral" argument I don't follow. It's a bit like the police saying they know a murderer comes from the south of England so they are going to execute everybody in Epsom.

Then again, why does Mr. Bush need to drop *three*

thousand bombs on Saddam Hussein? I would have thought one would have been enough to take him out, if he knows where Saddam is. And if he doesn't know where he is, what on earth is the moral justification for dropping any bombs at all? Doesn't Mr. Bush realize they are dangerous things and tend to kill people when they land?

Or does Mr. Bush simply enjoy the idea of taking out a lot of Iraqis?

I appreciate Mr. Bush's argument that because Saddam Hussein has refused to take any notice of the UN, Mr. Bush should teach him a lesson by dropping a lot of bombs on him. But now he's telling us that if the UN won't give him permission to do it, he's jolly well going to drop a lot of bombs on Saddam anyway. In which case, won't Mr. Bush be guilty of the same thing he's accusing Saddam Hussein of?

Apparently not because, according to the president's advisers, if the United Nations won't give him permission to drop a lot of bombs on Saddam Hussein, it will have ceased to be a "Responsible World Organization" and, therefore, he doesn't need to take any notice of it.

But, doesn't the same thing go for Saddam Hussein? If the United Nations ceases to be a "Responsible World Organization" how can the fact that Saddam Hussein has refused to take any notice of it be something so evil that it justifies dropping bombs on the poor people living under his heel?

And that's another thing—everyone seems to be very certain that dropping a lot of bombs on Baghdad will get rid of Saddam Hussein. But will it? Any more than devastating Afghanistan (and killing maybe twenty thousand people) got rid of Al Qaeda? A recent UN report reckons that if and when the U.S. starts bombing, as many as one hundred thousand Iraqis may die.

I can't really believe that the president of the United States gets his rocks off by having people killed. That's more like Saddam Hussein.

And yet it worries me that Mr. Bush says that one of the reasons he wants to kill a lot of Iraqis is because Saddam Hussein has also been killing them. Is there some sort of rivalry here?

Saddam's best time was back in 1988 when he killed several thousand at once, in the village of Halabja. Since then he's been carrying on the good work, but on a piecemeal basis. In fact, for all I know, since his 1988 spree, he may not have killed any more of his own citizens than George W. Bush did as governor of Texas.

When Mr. Bush became governor in 1995, the average number of executions per year was 7.6. Mr. Bush succeeded in quadrupling this to a magnificent 31.6 per year. He must have had the terrible chore of personally signing over 150 death warrants while he was governor. I suppose the advantage of killing Iraqis is that you don't have to sign a piece of paper for every one of them. Just one quick scribble and—bingo! You can kill a hundred thousand and no questions asked! What's more, nobody is going to quibble about some of them being mentally retarded or juveniles, which is what happened to George W. Bush when he was governor of Texas.

I'm not saying that George W. Bush shouldn't be allowed to kill as many people as he wants. After all, he is the unelected leader of the most powerful country on earth, so if he can't do anything he likes, who can?

What's more, you can bet that if George W. Bush is going for the record he's going to beat Saddam Hussein hands down.

And, in the years to come, we can confidently look forward to a lot more killing all over the world—certainly a lot more than Saddam Hussein ever managed in his own country.

RESPECT MY OIL HABIT, YOU ROGUE MOFO!
©Steve Bell 2003·1860·7·1·

15.

POOR TONY BLAIR WAKES UP

March 14, 2003

It's not easy when you find out that your friends have been using you as a chump.

Tony Blair must have been really sick this week when Donald Rumsfeld casually let drop that Mr. Bush and his team couldn't give a toss about Britain sending soldiers to Iraq. Truth is, they'd probably prefer it if we didn't, but our participation at least means they can pretend it's an international force.

But I bet Tony feels terribly slighted—after all he's gone through to prove his devotion to the ideals of extremist Republican militarism. He's practically split his party, put his own leadership in jeopardy, and made himself look thoroughly ill in the process. And what has he got out of it? A few pats on the back and a nice Christmas card from the White House, I expect.

I mean it's simply not fair. Here he is—prime minister of Great Britain (just)—and he's doing everything he possibly can, including leaning over backward and licking his own bottom. He's spending vast amounts of money he hasn't got on sending men to the Gulf. He's put his entire nation on the front line for terrorist reprisals. He's upset his other admirers in Europe, and—to cap it all off—he's put his name to a plan that is not just plain stupid but is actually wicked, and in return? Zilch.

All the contracts for reconstructing Iraq are to go to American companies—preferably ones like Haliburton, which is still paying Vice President Dick Cheney a fat $1 million a year for looking after their interests. But not a single British company is to benefit from all the mayhem and destruction that the bombing is going to cause.

Poor old Tony doesn't even get a bone.

I suppose he should have been more careful about who he was playing with in the first place.

But they took him for a sucker.

He thought he'd be able to cut a decent figure as the elder statesman, sagely steering his impetuous American friends away from actions they would later regret. And for that he was prepared to subscribe to the most hawkish, aggressive regime that has ever held power in the good ol' U.S. of A; a regime whose planners spelled out their schemes for American military world domination in a report for the Project for the New American Century published in September 2000, before George W. Bush seized power. (You can look it up on the Web at www.newamericancentury.org.)

Their aim, they say in their report, is "to shape a new century favorable to American principles and interests." And they make it quite clear that they envisage achieving those aims not by diplomacy but through military might, for which reason they need to "increase defense spending gradually to a minimum level of 3.5 to 3.8 percent of gross national product, adding $15 billion to $20 billion to total defense spending annually."

At the time, they knew there was little hope of the American public buying into such imperialistic dreams. What was needed, they said in their pre-September 11 report, was "some catastrophic and catalyzing event like a new Pearl Harbor." Well, their dreams came true.

And now it's quite obvious that instead of Mr. Rumsfeld and Mr. Cheney listening attentively to Mr. Blair's sage advice, they've simply been using him as a patsy—a convenient fig leaf.

Tony Blair has merely been helping to give Mr. Bush's

barbaric planners for world domination credibility among the American public.

The only conceivable hope of stopping their militaristic global ambitions is for the rest of the world to oppose them. There might then be some hope that the American public would wake up to what sort of a government they currently have.

The reawakening of American democracy is the only hope for a future world that is not ridden by terrorism and global warfare.

16.

TONY AND THE PIXIES

March 22, 2003

Dear Tony,

I'm terribly worried that you may be losing your grip on reality.

For example, a few days ago you went on television and announced that after the U.S. has bombed Baghdad, "We shall help Iraq move toward democracy."

Now, I don't want to be a wet blanket, Tony, but was it a leprechaun who suggested this idea to you?

Since the Second World War, the U.S. has bombed China, Korea, Guatemala, Indonesia, Cuba, Guatemala (again), Peru, Laos, Vietnam, Cambodia, Guatemala (third time lucky), Grenada, Lebanon, Libya, El Salvador,

Nicaragua, Iran, Panama, Iraq, Kuwait, Somalia, Bosnia, Afghanistan, and Yugoslavia—in that order—and in not a single case did the bombing produce a democratic government as a direct result.

Why do you think it will be any different in Iraq? Or did your fairy godmother promise you this along with a golden coach?

In the same TV appearance you also went a bit dreamy and said that you were going to "put the money from Iraqi oil in a UN trust fund so that it benefits Iraq and no one else."

Hasn't anyone told you that they've been debating how to use the Iraqi oil field money in the White House for months, and there is a strong body of opinion that thinks it's a good idea to use it to cover the expense of the U.S. military operation, which, let's face it, is going to be colossal. Six billion to nine billion dollars a month—that's a lot of money for a nation in the economic mess George W. Bush's America is currently in.

And then what on earth did you say to that nice Clare Short to persuade her not to resign? She came out of your office saying that you'd "persuaded President Bush that there must be a UN resolution on creating a UN mandate for the reconstruction of Iraq."

Now, come on! You've been playing with the pixies haven't you? You know perfectly well that President Bush and his people don't give a goblin's cuss for the UN.

Richard Perle, who happens to be chairman of Mr.

Bush's defense policy board, only this week called the UN "the chatterbox on the Hudson"—despite the fact that it's on the East River. (Hope his geography is a bit more accurate when *he* starts ordering the bombing!)

Perle was penning an obituary for the United Nations and he didn't seem too sad to see it go. "What will die is the fantasy of the UN as the foundation of a new world order . . . the liberal conceit of safety through international law administered by international institutions."

And what will replace the UN, in Mr. Perle's fairy-tale world? Why, the good ol' USA, of course! It will administer worldwide justice and punishment in the interests of "a new century favorable to American principles and interests." Not much comfort there for us elves and brownies.

You know, Mr. Bush and his advisors can't wait to sell the UN building off as luxury apartments with stunning views of the East River—sorry, Richard!—the Hudson. (I'm sure they're going to swap the names so as to bring the chairman of the defense policy board's remarks in line with reality.)

And, Tony, I hope you didn't persuade Clare to stay in your government by promising that she could be in charge of all the UN reconstruction and humanitarian aid, because you know that's only going to happen in dreamland.

Mr. Bush and his chums want this to be an exclusively U.S. business. They're only allowing American companies to bid for the £640 million worth of reconstruction planned (paid for, no doubt, by Iraqi oil) and that includes running the health and education services. Poor Clare is going to have a big empty office and nothing to do in it.

What's more, the UN won't continue its humanitarian aid (that currently feeds 60 percent of Iraqis) because the yanks will insist on U.S. troops delivering it. Washington boasts that its soldiers, when they've killed enough people, will magically transform into kindly aid workers. But Justin Forsyth, the head of policy at Oxfam says: "We don't want our aid equipment to be off-loaded off the back of a U.S. military lorry, because if we were to do that we would be seen as part of a belligerent force."

So, all little Clare Short will have got for compromising her principles and making herself a laughingstock is a short trip to Washington and somebody else's hanky to blow her nose in.

And I bet you don't make her deputy prime minister in the next reshuffle.

Now, I can't believe that you have done any of this deliberately. It must be those fairy folk, whispering in your ear. So, why don't you look into your heart and see if there is any glimmer of truth and honor left in there, and then chase those goblins and elves away. It could just work.

Best wishes,
Terry Jones

17.

WHAT WILL YOU SAY WHEN IT'S OVER, MR. BLAIR?

April 6, 2003

What will Mr. Blair say to us, when they've finished this shameful thing? When thousands and thousands of Iraqi citizens are dead will he still tell us it was worth it all to get rid of Saddam Hussein?

When more and more—maybe millions—of Iraqis have died through lack of clean water and lack of food, will Mr. Blair still tell us how keenly he feels for the people of Iraq?

When thousands of babies are dead in their mothers' arms from dysentery, will Mr. Blair still say it was better than letting the weapons inspectors carry on?

When the Americans have taken over the government of Iraq, or have established some neo-Saddam to rule in their interests, will Mr. Blair still tell us that we had to invade to make the Iraqi people free?

When Mr. Bush's regime starts using the money from Iraqi oil fields to pay for the damage our bombs have done to their country, will Mr. Blair still claim it was for the good of the Iraqi people?

When Mr. Bush has established a "permanent force presence" in the Gulf, which his advisors described as their real objective in September 2000, will Mr. Blair still claim this was worth the deaths of British troops?

Surely there will come a time, when even Mr. Blair will have to stop lying to his own people?

When it turns out that yet another assertion of British soldiers "executed" rather than killed in combat is untrue, will Mr. Blair apologize to the families?

When the UN has been scrapped or turned into another version of Oxfam, will Mr. Blair still claim the bombing was in the interests of world peace?

When terrorist attacks become so commonplace that American and British citizens become fearful of going about their daily business, will Mr. Blair still claim that he has acted to make us safer?

When you and I have to think twice about getting on a plane, and airlines have collapsed all over the world, will

Mr. Blair tell us it's solely the fault of some new Saddam or Osama?

When the Middle East has become a tinderbox of conflict, will Mr. Blair keep telling us he had no other choice of action?

When the Islamic world turns on the Christians and seeks revenge for the deeds now being done in Iraq, will Mr. Blair still bleat about the evil of Saddam Hussein?

When hundreds of Iraqis are being tortured in Guantánamo Bay without rights and without hope and in contradiction of the Geneva Convention, will Mr. Blair still insist that it is Britain's moral duty to support the jingoistic warmongers who currently run the White House?

When it becomes apparent—as it will—that Mr. Blair has put our soldiers on the battlefield to be killed solely in pursuit of the imperialist dreams of Donald Rumsfeld, Dick Cheney, and George Bush, will he still have the face to remain prime minister?

When it becomes clear that the only way Mr. Blair could have influenced the current U.S. administration was by opposing its plans for world domination, and by supporting those many Americans who resent the extremist regime under which they now are forced to live, will Mr. Blair still claim that he has any grasp on reality?

When we finally know the total score of Iraqi women and children maimed, mutilated, and blown to bits by

British and American forces in this hypocritical adventure, will Mr. Blair be able to look at his ravaged face in the mirror without wanting to slit his wrists?

Surely there will come a time when even Mr. Blair will have to stop lying to his own conscience—let alone his own people?

18.

IT'S TIME FOR CONGRATULATIONS

April 10, 2003

Well, the war's been a huge success, and I guess it's time for congratulations all 'round. And, wow! It's hard to know where to begin.

First, I'd like to congratulate Kellogg, Brown & Root and the Bechtel Group, who are the construction companies most likely to benefit from the reconstruction of Iraq. Contracts in the region of $1 billion should soon be coming your way, boys. Well done! And, what with the U.S. dropping 15,000 precision-guided munitions, 7,500 unguided bombs, and 750 cruise missiles on Iraq so far and with more to come, there's going to be a lot of reconstruction to do. It looks like it could be a bonanza year!

Of course, we all know that Kellogg, Brown & Root are the construction side of Halliburton, and they've been doing big business with the military ever since the Second World War. Most recently they got the plum job of constructing the prison compound for terrorist suspects at Guantánamo Bay. Could be a whole lot more deluxe chicken coops coming your way in the next few months, guys! Stick it to 'em!

I'd also like to add congratulations to Dick Cheney, who was chief executive of Halliburton from 1995 to 2000, and who currently receives a check for $1 million a year from his old company. I guess he may find there's a little surprise bonus in there this year. Well done, Dick! And congratulations.

Congratulations, too, to former Secretary of State George Shultz. He's not only on the board of Bechtel, he's also chairman of the advisory board of the Committee for the Liberation of Iraq—a group with close ties to the White House committed to reconstructing the Iraqi economy through war. You're doing a grand job, George, and I'm sure material benefits will be coming your way, as sure as the Devil lives in Texas.

Oh, and before I forget, a big round of appreciation for Jack Sheehan, a retired general who sits on the Defense Policy Board that advises the Pentagon. He's a senior vice president at Bechtel and one of the many members of the Defense Policy

Board with links to companies that make money out of defense contracts—and when I say "make money" I'm not joking! Their companies have benefited to the tune of $76 billion just in the last year! Talk about a gravy train! Well, Jack, you and your colleagues can certainly look forward to a warm and joyous Christmas this year!

It's been estimated that rebuilding Iraq could cost anything from $25 billion to $100 billion and the great thing is that the Iraqis will be paying for it themselves out of their future oil revenues! What's more, President Bush will be able to say, with a straight face, that they're using the money from Iraqi oil to benefit the Iraqi people! "We're going to use the assets of the people of Iraq, especially their oil assets, to benefit their people," said Secretary of State Colin L. Powell, and he looked really sincere! Yessir! It's so neat it makes you want to run out and buy shares in Fluor! As one of the world's biggest procurement and construction companies, they recently hired Kenneth J. Oscar who, as acting assistant secretary of the army, took care of the Pentagon's $35 billion-a-year procurement budget. So there could also be some nice extra business coming their way soon! Good for them! Congratulations!

But every celebration has its serious side, and I should like to convey my condolences to all those who have suffered so grievously in this war, particularly American Airlines, Qantas, and Air Canada, and all other travel companies who have seen their customers dwindle, as fear of terrorist reprisals for what the U.S. and Britain have done in Iraq begins to bite.

My condolences also to all those British companies who have been disappointed in their bid to share in the bonanza that all this wonderful high-tech military fire-power has created. I know it must be frustrating and disheartening for many of you, especially those in the medical field, knowing there are all those severed limbs, all that burnt flesh, all those smashed skulls, broken bones, punctured spleens, ripped faces, and mangled children just crying out for your products. You could be making a fortune out of the drugs and serums and surgical hardware, and yet you have to stand by on the sidelines and watch as U.S. drug companies make a killing.

Well, Hosni Mubarak, the Egyptian president, has some words of comfort for us all. As he recently pointed out, this adventure of Bush and Blair's will have created such hatred throughout the Arab world, that a hundred new bin Ladens will have been created. So all of us here in Britain as well as in America shouldn't lose heart. Once the Arab world starts to take its revenge, there should be enough reconstruction to do at home to keep business thriving for some years to come.

19.

A ~~SACRED~~ SCARED PROPHET

April 25, 2003

"I can see the future."

"How were you blessed with this mystic ability, O Prophetic One?"

"I received my gift through watching George W. Bush on *NBC News*."

"What does this gift tell you of the future, O Prophetic One?"

"I see U.S. weapons inspectors touring Iraq and discovering chemical or biological weapons of mass destruction in convincing quantities."

"Does your gift tell you how the U.S. weapons inspectors find them when the UN inspectors failed?"

"No, but I see a White House spokesman saying, 'The U.S. inspectors have been told where to look by captured "human Iraqis"'—to use George W. Bush's telling phrase. I see Donald Rumsfeld assuring us that anything the U.S. does will be much more efficient than anything the UN does."

"What does 'efficient' mean, O Prophetic One?"

"It means 'helpful to the plans of Donald Rumsfeld.' What else could 'efficient' mean, O Tiny-Brained Picker of Other People's Noses?"

"What else does the future hold?"

"I see Jack Straw with a dreadful smirk on his face. I see Anthony Blair with a dreadful smirk on his face. I see them both holding endless press conferences in which they repeat: 'We told you so!' over and over again. On the other hand, I see many people thinking that the U.S. weapons inspectors did not learn anything from the captured 'human Iraqis' and that the U.S. inspectors themselves have planted the Weapons of Mass Destruction specifically so that Jack Straw and Anthony Blair can hold press conferences and say, 'We told you so.'"

"But surely no one can really believe that where the UN inspectors failed to find Weapons of Mass Destruction the U.S. inspectors really have found some?"

"I see Jack Straw and Anthony Blair repeating, 'We told you so' so often that it doesn't matter. The finding of the Weapons of Mass Destruction becomes a 'fact' that is endlessly repeated in the press until everyone forgets that the people who found the Weapons of Mass Destruction had a vested interest in finding them. In fact, if they hadn't found them they would be liable to prosecution as war criminals."

"But if Iraq had these weapons why didn't they use them?"

"I see a White House spokesman telling journalists that Iraq didn't use its WMD because it was too scared and that shows that it was right to bomb them. No, wait! There is another press conference! In this one the White House spokesman is saying that the U.S. military strike was so fast and effective that the Iraqis simply didn't get the chance to use their WMD."

"And do the people believe such rubbish, O Prognosticator of Political Poppycock?"

"What people really believe doesn't matter. It's how you get them to conform that matters. That's what worked for Saddam Hussein and there's no reason why it shouldn't work for George W. Bush."

"What does your gift of prophecy tell you about the UN's role in the rebirth of Iraq, O Gifted Seer?"

"I see a 'For Sale' sign hanging outside the UN building on the East River. I see another sign on the same building. It says: 'Trump Casino Resort.' I see an office somewhere in Boston; outside a sign reads: 'Oxfam America—Now incorporating the United Nations.'"

"But surely George W. Bush promised Anthony Blair that the UN would play a 'central role' in the future Iraq."

"That was in Belfast, O Brain of a Christmas Turkey without the Stuffing. No promises made in Belfast mean anything."

"What else do you . . ."

"I see us spending on the military rising to 3.5 and 3.9 percent of the GNP. I see the U.S. waging 'multiple simultaneous large-scale wars.' I see U.S. planes making preemptive strikes on any nation that might threaten American superiority. I see the U.S. destroying any ballistic missiles and WMD that might 'allow lesser states to deter U.S. military action by threatening U.S. allies and the American homeland itself.'"

"O Far Seeing One! You could tell all this simply from seeing George W. Bush interviewed on *NBC News*?"

"No, I was quoting from 'Rebuilding America's Defenses,' the blueprint for the present U.S. government's foreign policy. And, blessed as I am with the gift of foresight, it scares the shit out of me."

20.

IF FISH FEEL PAIN . . .

May 2, 2003

The recent report by the Royal Society suggesting that fish can feel pain will come as a severe blow to all those anglers who have hitherto operated on the principle that fish are incapable of feeling anything. It comes as an even bigger shock to those of us who have for so long applied the same principle to human beings.

If fish can feel pain, does this mean that a thirteen-year-old child, picked up in Afghanistan, hooded, flown several thousand miles to Cuba and kept in a chicken coop, may also experience physical sensations bordering on the uncomfortable? Like Tony Blair, I thought the

Guantánamo Bay camp was "an unsatisfactory situation," but it never occurred to me that the human beings in there would be capable of feeling discomfort.

In much the same way, I suppose, George W. Bush must have assumed that all those prisoners on death row, whose death sentences he signed as governor, would never undergo distress at the prospect of imminent death. Like him, I always firmly believed that human beings were incapable of feeling any unpleasantness.

Otherwise, I used to point out, why would civilized people like Donald Rumsfeld even contemplate dropping cluster bombs all over the Middle East where kids will pick them up or tread on them and get blown to pieces or have their legs ripped off? If fish can feel, there must be a strong possibility that small Iraqi children will be unhappy at losing bits of their bodies.

If fish can feel, perhaps we should rethink some of our other policies. I mean maybe it's not such a good idea to dump mentally ill people on the streets in the hope that some passersby will give them "community care"? Just suppose that—like fish—the mentally ill can feel miserable? At least there is no suggestion that fish suffer from the cold and wet, so there's no problem in leaving the mentally ill out on the streets through the winter, but that's not the point. The point is that we ought to reexamine some of our long-held and most cherished assumptions.

Like, for example, the idea that being out of work is just something that happens to some schmucks but has no bearing on their quotient of personal contentment. If fish can feel, maybe George W. Bush should be more worried about the U.S. unemployment rate reaching 6 percent than about how fabulous it is that his military can drop so many bombs and fire off so many missiles in such a short time.

If fish can feel, perhaps Tony Blair should reconsider his support for a U.S. administration that is publicly pledged to visiting war and destruction on any other country that dares to oppose them. If fish can feel, perhaps we ought not to allow the men and women who currently run the White House to run the world in the way that they clearly intend.

If fish can feel pain, perhaps it's time to govern human affairs on the principle that human beings feel pain, too.

21.

TRUTH—THE ULTIMATE TERRORIST WEAPON

May 16, 2003

Terrorism has entered a new era. It has become clear over the last week that terrorists have targeted leading politicians with their latest weapon: a biological truth drug that forces well-known figures to blurt out what they are really thinking.

These truth attacks have already claimed as victim Clare Short, who was unable to stop herself standing up in Parliament and confessing that "those who are wielding power are not accountable and are not scrutinized."

Another target has been David Blunkett, the home secretary, who found himself unaccountably blabbing to the

Police Federation about his loathing of judges and his utter contempt for the whole legal apparatus of which he is head. And then Oliver Letwin, the shadow home secretary, was moved to make a clean breast of his belief that only a miracle could save the Tory Party from defeat at the next election.

In each of these cases the terrorists obviously went for vulnerable, easy targets.

However, it is reported that the next truth attacks could target the prime minister. This has caused widespread alarm throughout the cabinet. Ministers fear that if Tony Blair were to suddenly blurt out the true depths of his despair, now he realizes what the Bush administration's role for him is, it could jeopardize his ability to lead the Labor Party into the next election.

But there is worse to come. Imagine the effect on voters, if the prime minister were to make public the guilt he must now be feeling at having lied through his teeth for all those months about Iraq's Weapons of Mass Destruction. And just suppose he starts blabbering about his remorse, as a Christian, for every single child, woman, and man now dead, or mutilated as a result of his having bombed a country that was no conceivable threat to the UK.

Or, what if he were suddenly to confess that he had once had delusions of being a moderating influence on the hawks in the U.S. administration, but he now realizes he was as foolish in believing *them* as Clare Short was in believing *him*?

On the other side of the Atlantic, however, there is less concern about the effects of a truth attack, since the objectives of the current regime are already public knowledge.

Of course, a few eyebrows might be raised if George W. Bush were to disclose what he would have actually done to the UK if it hadn't supported his ambitions in the Middle East.

Similarly, there might be some fallout if Donald Rumsfeld, James Woolsey, Dick Cheney, Richard Perle, George Shultz, and the rest took it upon themselves to advertise how much money they're all hoping to make out of the upcoming wars they're proposing and out of all the antiterrorist security their companies will be providing.

But their desire to run the world in their interests and to attack any country that they regard as a threat to those interests has been known to everyone (apart from the prime minster of Great Britain) for some time.

That is why, perhaps, the terrorists are not at present targeting a truth attack on the U.S. The American public seems to be untroubled by the corruption of its government and unconcerned by its leaders' plans for starting a new age of global warfare.

In such an environment, I suppose, the truth simply doesn't matter anymore.

22.

ALASTAIR CAMPBELL AND THE DEVIL

July 4, 2003

The British government's communications director attacked the BBC for daring to suggest that Tony Blair had "sexed-up" the government's dossier on Iraq—particularly by including the detail that Iraq could assemble a nuclear attack in forty-five minutes.

The Devil wants to know how he could improve his image in the world. So, he visits Alastair Campbell.

"Simple," says the British government's communications director. "All you've got to do is demonstrate that it's not you who is the root of all evil but God."

"I'm never going to be able to persuade people to believe that," replies the Devil. "Look at all the great things he's given them. And everybody knows he tells the truth."

"Leave it to me," said Alastair Campbell.

So, Alastair Campbell rings up God and says, "Hi, God!"

"Don't you 'Hi God!' me you two-timing, weasel-mouthed fabricator of pork pies!"

"God! I'm ringing you on behalf of the Devil. He says you've been running him down in public recently."

"Right!" says God. "He's a bad lot that Devil. He goes 'round telling lies and starting wars. Look at this latest business in Iraq."

"Now, you can't blame the Devil for that," says Alastair Campbell. "Everyone knows it was Saddam Hussein's fault. He was a threat to world peace."

"Come on!" says God. "You don't believe that!"

"What I believe doesn't matter. Can you prove it was the Devil's doing."

"Sure!" says God. "He got the American people to believe Saddam Hussein was somehow responsible for September 11, and he got the British to believe Saddam was about to bomb them. He made it all up."

"Are you sure?" asks Alastair Campbell.

"Well, of course he made it all up. September 11 was Osama bin Laden's doing and he hates Saddam Hussein.

Saddam may be a nasty piece of work but he had nothing to do with flying planes into the World Trade Center.

"As for Saddam being about to attack the UK—that's the most ludicrous proposition I've ever heard. What possible reason could he have had for bombing the UK? Military advantage? Economic advantage? Political advantage? Territorial advantage? Come on! You know it's ridiculous! And even if he had, he could be sure he'd have been wiped off the face of the earth as a result."

So, Alastair Campbell goes back to the Devil and tells him what God said.

"It's all true," moans the Devil. "I did all those things. You know God tells the truth. It's so unfair—God's omnipotent and omniscient and omnipresent, and I'm just the Devil. I always lose out."

"Okay," says Alastair Campbell. "Leave it to me."

So, Alastair Campbell issues a statement accusing God of lying by saying that the Devil had made-up the story about Saddam Hussein being about to bomb the UK within forty-five minutes.

"The Devil didn't make that bit up," says Alastair Campbell. "He had it from the Security Services."

God is beside himself with rage. He calls in his lawyers and tells them to sue Alastair Campbell, but the lawyers say they're too scared of Alastair Campbell.

Meanwhile, Alastair Campbell allows a document to

be leaked proving that the Devil was merely repeating what the Security Services told him about the forty-five minutes.

An almighty row blows up, in which Alastair Campbell attacks God for lying, for misleading the British public and for bringing religion into disrepute.

The forty-five minutes becomes the big issue. Was God lying when he said the Devil insisted on including the forty-five minutes? Or did the Devil insist on including it against the wishes of the Security Services?

It's all totally irrelevant to whether or not Saddam Hussein bombed the Twin Towers or was a threat to the UK, but now nobody can think about anything else.

In the end, God rings up the Devil.

"I'm sorry, God," whines the Devil. "It's not my fault."

"Shut up!" says God. "You're fired!"

"Don't say that!" says the Devil. "Who are you going to get to do all the stuff I have to do?"

"Alastair Campbell," says God. "I'm very impressed with the way he's handled this whole thing."

"God!" says the Devil. "You're wicked!"

23.

THE REAL REASONS WHY TONY BLAIR SHOULD RESIGN

August 8, 2003

Andrew Gilligan was the BBC reporter who claimed that Alastair Campbell "sexed-up" the dossier on Iraq.

So, Tony Blair considers his only reason for resigning would be if Andrew Gilligan's story that Alastair Campbell inserted the forty-five-minute claim was true.

Well, if it's any help, Tony, I can think of a lot of other reasons why you could resign.

You might consider resigning because you lied about your part in outing Dr. Kelly. I don't suppose you remember, but on the plane from Shanghai to Hong Kong, July 21, 2003, you told reporters that you "emphatically" did not authorize the leak. Hard to know quite how you *don't* do something "emphatically" but that's what you said. To the Hutton inquiry, however, you admitted overall "responsibility" for the decision to announce that a government official had admitted talking to the BBC's Andrew Gilligan. Now, you might say that was not "authorizing the leak"—but then, from what I understand, Hitler never gave orders to build the extermination camps—it's just his subordinates knew it was what he'd want. Same with Henry II and the murder of Thomas Becket, I suppose.

You could also resign on the grounds of incapability. After all, anybody who actually thought that Iraq was an imminent threat to the UK obviously hasn't got much grasp on reality. Was Iraq about to bomb London? Did Saddam Hussein have designs on occupying Gibraltar or perhaps East Cheam? Wasn't he rather preoccupied with keeping himself in power in his own country? But then I suppose you've got more sympathy for the Iraqi dictator's position nowadays.

Or, why not resign on the grounds of mismanagement? I mean you have tolerated unbelievable incompetence in your intelligence agencies. Sir John Scarlett told the Hutton inquiry that he knew of not a single intelligence officer who had any doubts about the September dossier. Well, we now know that at least one of his officers, Dr. Kelly, had such grave doubts that he told the press about them. If Sir John Scarlett doesn't know what's going on in his own department he can't be much of a spymaster can he?

And, then again, if not a single intelligence officer doubted the September dossier, why in heavens didn't they? We now know the thing to be total nonsense. Iraq had no Weapons of Mass Destruction, no nuclear capability, didn't buy uranium from Nigeria, and couldn't assemble nuclear weapons in forty-five minutes—it's all rubbish. So why didn't any of our so-called intelligence officers realize it was rubbish? Are they so out of touch with what's actually happening out there? Maybe we should close the intelligence services down and spend the money on something useful, like making movies.

In fact, while you're at it, you might also consider resigning on the grounds of your own ineptitude. After all, your policies regarding Iraq have resulted in the exact opposite of what you claimed they would do. You said that by bombing Iraq you were going to bring Iraqis a better way of life. Yet your policies have actually resulted in the destruction of Iraq's infrastructure. They have meant millions of Iraqis have had to endure the summer without proper supplies of water and without electricity. They have brought chaos and lawlessness and misery to the country.

You also promised your policies were going to bring freedom to Iraq. But this week, the U.S. supremo in Baghdad introduced a regime of political witch-hunting. Thousands of decent, law-abiding Iraqis, lawyers, doctors, and university professors now find themselves thrown out of their jobs because they had once belonged to the Ba'athist Party. That's not freedom in any sense of the word as I understand it, Tony.

You also claimed you wanted to make the world a safer place and to stamp out terrorism. Now call me naive, but I'm prepared to take a bet with you that there are now thousands—if not millions—more potential terrorists in Iraq and in the Arab world in general as a direct result of your obsession with dropping bombs on a defenseless country.

These are all much better reasons for resigning than what a BBC reporter might have said.

Or, you could resign because of unsuitability for the post. I mean, at any moment, you could be charged as a war criminal—certainly by any definition that the UN has to offer. You personally authorized the dropping of bombs on another country when your own nation was under no threat of attack from that country. You've also been responsible for the killing of somewhere in the region of forty thousand Iraqi civilians and soldiers (mostly wretched conscripts). Personally, I don't like being governed by a man with blood on his hands or who may one day have to go and answer questions in the Hague.

Or, why not resign over the general fact that you misled Parliament and the country into thinking that Iraq was an imminent threat to the UK? That's more to the point than whether Alastair Campbell inserted the forty-five-minutes line or not.

Or, how about resigning on the grounds that you are already no longer actually running this country anyway? It's quite obvious to anyone (who is not in politics) that you simply do whatever it is that George W. Bush's advisers tell you to do.

I mean, do you think we're stupid? How come the only people in the world who thought Iraq was a threat were you and George Bush? And we know he didn't really. His advisors, Cheney, Perle, Wolfowitz, etc. had been planning to invade Iraq since at least September 2000 when they publicly announced that Iraq was a top target for American aggression should they ever get into power. In their seminal document, "Rebuilding America's Defenses," they wrote, "The United States has for decades sought to play a more permanent role in Gulf regional security. While the unresolved conflict with Iraq provides the immediate justification, the need for a substantial American force presence in the Gulf transcends the issue of the regime of Saddam Hussein."

So my advice, Tony, is resign now regardless of whether Andrew Gilligan got it right or not, and simply let Bush, Cheney, Perle, and the rest of that gang take over running the UK.

It'll be more honest in the end than forty thousand of your smiles.

24.

WHY TONY WENT TO WAR

October 4, 2003

In his historic speech to the Labor Party conference, at Bournemouth, the prime minister made an impassioned plea for those who attacked his decision to invade Iraq to "at least understand why I took it and why I would take the same decision again."

He then offered us his reasons. And, since it is of some importance to understand why our prime minister took this country into an unpopular and widely opposed invasion of another sovereign state, it is worth quoting him at length:

"Imagine you are prime minister and you receive this

intelligence. And not just about Iraq. But about the whole murky trade in WMD. And one thing we know—not from intelligence, but from historical fact—that Saddam's regime has not just developed but used such weapons gassing thousands of his own people. And has lied about it consistently, concealing it for years even under the noses of the UN inspectors.

"And I see the terrorism and the trade in WMD growing. And I look at Saddam's country and I see its people in torment ground underfoot by his and his sons' brutality and wickedness. So, what do I do? Say 'I've got the intelligence but I've a hunch its wrong?' Leave Saddam in place but now with the world's democracies humiliated and him emboldened?"

So, let me get this straight, because, as one of the millions who opposed invading Iraq, I'm keen to understand why Tony took that decision.

First he received "some intelligence." Apparently, whatever this "intelligence" was it wasn't just about Iraq. Fair enough, although if it wasn't about Iraq you wonder what its relevance is to dropping bombs on Iraqis. Anyway, it turns out there was another piece of "intelligence" (as opposed to the first bit of intelligence) and this was about a "trade" in Weapons of Mass Destruction. However, the prime minister doesn't know much about this trade because all he tells us about it is that it is "murky."

So far I don't quite see how any of this has any bearing on his decision to attack Iraq. Doubtless he is about to explain. But, wait a minute!

Suddenly the prime minister of Great Britain is very keen to bring us onto firmer ground. Let's forget about vague things like "intelligence" or some "murky" trade that we don't know much about. Let's get down to a solid fact—"one thing we know"—something based not on "intelligence" but on "historical fact." We can trust this one. This must be the key reason for going to war.

And what is it? It's that Saddam Hussein has gassed thousands of his own people. And not only that. He's lied about it!

So, that's why Tony Blair decided to drop bombs on the Iraqi people—because Saddam Hussein gassed them twelve years ago.

But Tony's explanation of why he bombed Iraq isn't over yet. He tells us: *"I see the terrorism and the trade in WMD growing."* And how is this connected to Iraq? He elucidates: *"And I look at Saddam's country and I see its people in torment ground underfoot by his and his sons' brutality and wickedness."* The only connection Tony offers us is that he *sees* all these three things.

Simple as that! Tony *sees* terrorism, he *sees* WMD, and he *sees* Saddam's brutality and hey, presto! Without troubling to make any other connection between them he decides to invade Iraq.

Of course, he makes no connections between terrorism, WMD, and invading Iraq because there is none.

But there is another connection. In invading Iraq, Tony Blair has done the opposite of what he claims he intends to do in all three spheres.

In invading Iraq, he has increased the threat of global terrorism—in fact, his intelligence agencies advised him that would happen before he decided to drop his bombs.

In invading Iraq, he has done nothing to stop "the murky trade in WMD." Iraq has never been a seller of arms; it has always been a buyer. It is Britain and the U.S. who are the murky traders.

In invading Iraq, he has replaced the brutality of Saddam with the brutality of an uncomprehending invading army. He has replaced the repression of Saddam Hussein with lawlessness and chaos.

As someone who attacks his decision to invade a country that was no conceivable threat to Britain, I *do* now understand why Tony Blair took his decision. By his own account he took it for no good reason at all—other than the vacuous, incoherent ramblings of a demagogue.

25.

LORD HUTTON AND THE EMPEROR

January 29, 2004

The Hutton Inquiry into the death of a British government weapons expert curiously focused on the allegations made by Andrew Gilligan that Blair had "sexed-up" the dossier on Iraq. Hutton totally exonerated the government and condemned the BBC for failing to effectively control its reporters. The report was generally dismissed as a whitewash.

Lord Hutton has finally published his long-awaited report into the Emperor's new clothes. Speculation in the media that the Emperor has been walking around stark naked for the last few months has finally been put to rest. Lord Hutton concludes that not only has there been no duplicity whatsoever on the part of the manufacturers of the clothes, but that there has been no hint of gullibility on the part of the Emperor or any of his ministers, officers of state, or, indeed anyone associated with the Emperor.

Indeed, Lord Hutton goes on to stress that it is perfectly obvious for all to see that the Emperor's new clothes are of excellent workmanship, that they have been cut to fit the Emperor perfectly and that they are made of the very finest materials, including top-quality satin with rare silk linings and intricate lace cuffs. The colors, he says, are remarkable—as is obvious to anyone who looks at the clothes—and the overall effect of the garments is a credit to the Emperor.

Lord Hutton confirms, beyond a shadow of doubt, the manufacturers' claim that the clothes are indeed only invisible to those "who are unfit for office or else just plain stupid." Everyone else, says Lord Hutton, can see the clothes with their own eyes and can appreciate what very fine clothes they are.

The Emperor has expressed his relief and his appreciation for Lord Hutton's painstaking investigation. In a public statement he challenged all those who have been going round accusing him of walking the corridors of power in the nude to come forward and apologize . . .

Singled out for particular criticism, in the report, is a small child who claimed that he could see the Emperor as naked as the day that he was born. Lord Hutton states that the child had no factual evidence for making this statement, and that the claim amounted to a "very grave" attack upon the credibility and dignity of the Emperor and, indeed, upon all his ministers of state and advisors.

The law lord goes on to condemn the child's parents, teachers, and relatives for failing to make a proper investigation into the child's statement before it was made. "In any society," Lord Hutton writes, "it is vital that children do not make false accusations of fact impugning the credibility of others, especially the Emperor. Where any child is intending to make statements that might bring the Emperor or any members of his staff into disrepute or make them the subject of ridicule, the parents and teachers of that child should ensure that a system is in place whereby they can give careful consideration to the wording of the child's statement and whether it is right in all the circumstances for the child to make the statement."

Lord Hutton states that steps should be taken to ensure that in the future no small children are allowed to make unsubstantiated statements of fact that could be detrimental to the Emperor that are not based on solid research and have been verified by a parliamentary subcommittee and by at least two law lords nominated by the Emperor.

Reaction to Lord Hutton's report has been divided. The Emperor's staff are said to be ecstatic, and the Emperor himself has stated that "the lie that I was walking around without any clothes on has now been proved to be the real lie." It is hard to remember when the Emperor was last seen to smile so much, since he has been suffering recently from the cold.

It remains to be seen, however, how many members of the Emperor's entourage will now take up wearing clothes made from the same material and whether or not the manufacturers will be able to persuade the general public to buy similar garments.

Outside the Emperor's immediate circle, reaction to the report has been more critical. Some fear that the long-term effect of Lord Hutton's work may be to bring into public disrepute the whole system of public inquiries and to reduce to a laughingstock the idea of getting an elderly law lord to turn a serious and important matter of public debate into an all-out attack on the Emperor's critics.

It may well be that the Hutton Report will mark a watershed in the people's belief in the way in which their country is run. There are those who say that it is one thing to see the Emperor himself walking about in his new clothes despite the fact that his teeth are chattering with the cold and his fingers are turning blue, but it is quite another to silence anyone who suggests that he should put on something warmer.

Perhaps we are about to enter into a new age in which no one is permitted to give voice to what they see with their own eyes for fear of bursting the bubble of deception that currently encompasses most of those who now govern us.

STANDING BY HIS INTELLIGENCE...
©Steve Bell 2003 - 1951. 15.7.03-

26.

GRADING TONY'S LATEST ESSAY

April 4, 2004

Dear Mr. and Mrs. Blair,

I have just had to grade Tony's essay, "Why We Must Never Abandon this Historic Struggle in Iraq," and I am extremely worried.

Your son has been in the sixth form* now for several years, studying world politics, and yet his recent essay shows so little grasp of the subject that I can only conclude he has spent most of that time staring out of the window.

*Twelfth grade in high school is the American equivalent.

His essay, of course, is written with his usual passion and conviction, but in the real world, passion and conviction do not count for many marks.

Crucially, Tony does not seem to have read any of the firsthand accounts that are easily available and that describe what is really going on in Iraq.

On the recent escalation in violence, for example, he writes, "The insurgents are former Saddam sympathizers . . . terrorist groups linked to Al Qaeda and, most recently, followers of . . . Muqtada-al-Sadr."

This is simply not good enough. Tony ignores the multitude of reports indicating that revulsion against the occupation is now widespread amongst ordinary people.

Tony's essay also displays a dismal ignorance of the key factors involved, such as Mr. Bremer's closing down of the small circulation newspaper run by Muqtada-al-Sadr.

To be honest, Tony seems to be totally unaware of what has been going on in Falluja. Back in June 2003, David Baran described how Falluja was a town at peace, until U.S. forces took over, opened depots to looters, established a military base in a school, and kept the residents under surveillance through binoculars—"a gross invasion of privacy in a conservative area, where women keep out of the sight of strangers."

When residents protested, the Americans responded with bullets and grenades, killing some of them. Tony cannot simply ignore these factors if he is to stand any chance of being taken seriously in his A-S levels.

In fact, I begin to wonder what goes on in the boy's head? Does he really believe that the six-hundred Iraqis whom the U.S. has now killed in revenge for the four "civilian contractors," were all "terrorists" or Ba'athist supporters, despite the fact that those manning the hospitals report that most of the casualties are women, children, or old men?

Tony's uncritical acceptance of information supplied by the U.S. reveals a naivety that would be surprising in any sixth-form pupil, let alone one who has hopes of going on to university and then government, as I know Tony does.

He writes, "On the one side, outside terrorists, an extremist who has created his own militia, and remnants of a brutal dictatorship. . . . On the other side, people of immense courage and humanity . . ."

This might do in the infants, but I'm afraid by the sixth-form we expect something a little more sophisticated.

He totally fails to place events in the larger political context, and seems to imagine that the U.S. intends to establish what he calls "a sovereign state, governed democratically by the Iraqi people" with "the wealth of that potentially rich country" becoming "their wealth."

Does he really think that an Iraqi government that has been handpicked by the neo-conservatives in the White

House is democratic? Does he really think that the 120,000 U.S. troops that will remain behind in Iraq will make it "a sovereign state"? And does he really think that the forcible selling off of Iraqi industry to foreign companies (mainly American) will help to keep the wealth for the Iraqi people?

I can only give Tony three out of ten for this current effort and must warn him to pull up his socks if he wishes to carry on in this subject.

To be quite candid, Mr. and Mrs. Blair, it's lucky that your son is not in a position of power; otherwise his lack of insight and his crass ignorance would place us all in appalling peril.

27

GEORGE W. BUSH'S LOBOTOMY

April 17, 2004

Everyone agrees that President George Bush's lobotomy has been a tremendous success.

Dick Cheney, the vice president, declared that he was fully satisfied with it from his point of view.

"Without the lobotomy," Mr. Cheney told the American Academy of Neurology, "it might have proved difficult to persuade the president to start wars all around the world without any good pretext. But the removal of those parts of the brain associated with understanding the outcome of one's actions has enabled the president to function fully and without hesitation. Even when it is clear that disaster is around the corner, as it is currently in Iraq, the chief executive is able to go on TV and announce that everything is on course and that he has no intention of changing tactics that have already proved disastrous.

"I would like to commend the surgeons, nurses, and all involved with the operation," said Mr. Cheney.

Similarly, Mr. Rumsfeld, regards the surgery as an unqualified success. He writes in this month's *American Medical Association Journal*:

"The president's prefrontal leucotomy has successfully removed all neural reflexes resistant to war-profiteering. It is a tribute to the medical team who undertook this delicate operation that, no matter how close the connection between those instigating military action and the companies who benefit from it, the president is able to carry on as if he were morally in the right."

Paul Wolfowitz, the deputy secretary of defense, is also delighted at the beneficial effect that medical intervention has had on the president's brain.

"Just imagine how the president might have responded to Ariel Sharon's crazy schemes if we hadn't had the foresight to take out the neural pathways normally connected with perception and understanding," Mr. Wolfowitz told a meeting of The Association of Muslim Neurosurgeons for an All-Jewish Israel. "The president is now capable of treating the man responsible for the massacres at Shatila and Sabra as a decent human being, whose advice on how to deal with the problems of Israel is not only worth listening to but taking."

With all this acclaim for the U.S. president's lobotomy, it is scarcely surprising that British premier, Tony Blair, should have decided to follow suit and undergo similar psychosurgery.

Thanks to the inhibition of specific presynaptic terminals, Mr. Blair now appears to feel totally comfortable giving his support to the U.S. massacre in Falluja and to the activities of U.S. snipers who have been so busy in that city shooting women, children, and ambulance drivers in revenge for the murder of four mercenaries.

It is also believed that intervention in the motor speech area of his cortex now enables Mr. Blair to describe Iraqis who respond negatively to having their houses blown up as "fanatics, extremists, and terrorists."

Similarly, ablation of the oculomotor nerve means that Mr. Blair is now able to see Israeli plans to retain Jewish settlements in the West Bank as a big step forward in the Middle East peace process.

What has come as a complete surprise, however, is the recent revelation that Mr. Blair's brain surgery may even predate President Bush's. For without the removal of large portions of his cerebellum, it is hard to understand how the British prime minister could have turned down Mr.

Bush's no-strings offer to keep British troops out of combat in Iraq.

Political commentators are thus finding it impossible to say whether it is Mr. Bush or Mr. Blair who has pioneered the use of executive lobotomies in the "War against Terrorism."

28.

THE WAR OF WORDS IN IRAQ

April 28, 2004

One of the chief problems with the current exciting adventure in Iraq is that no one can agree on what to call anyone else.

In the Second World War we were fighting the Germans and the Germans were fighting us. Everyone agreed who was fighting who. That's what a proper war is like.

But in Iraq, there isn't even any agreement on what to call the Americans. The Iraqis insist on calling them "Americans," which seems on the face of it reasonable. The Americans, however, insist on calling themselves

"Coalition Forces." This is probably the first time in history that the U.S. has tried to share its military glory with someone else.

Hollywood, for example, is forever telling us it was the Americans who won the Second World War. It was an American who led the breakout from Colditz in *The Great Escape*, the Americans who captured the Enigma machine in *U571*, and Tom Cruise who single-handedly won the Battle of Britain (in *The Few*).

So, I suppose it's reassuring to find the U.S. generals in Iraq so keen to emphasize the role played by America's partners in bringing a better way of life to Iraq.

Then there's the problem of what the Americans are going to call the Iraqis—especially the ones they kill. You can only call people who are defending their own homes from rockets and missiles launched from helicopters and tanks "fanatics and terrorists" for so long. Eventually even newspaper readers will smell a rat.

Similarly, it's fiendishly difficult to get people to accept the label "rebels" for those Iraqis killed by American snipers when—as in Falluja—they turn out to be pregnant women, thirteen-year-old boys, and old men standing by their front gates.

It also sounds a bit lame to call ambulance drivers "fighters"—when they've been shot through the windshield in the act of driving the wounded to the hospital—and yet what other word can you use without making them sound like illegitimate targets?

I hope you're beginning to see the problem.

The key thing, I suppose, is to try and call U.S. mercenaries "civilians" or "civilian contractors" while calling Iraqi civilians "fighters" or "insurgents."

Describing the recent attack on Najaf, the *New York Times* happily hit upon the word "militiamen." This has the advantage of being a bit vague (nobody really knows what a "militiaman" looks like or does) while at the same time sounding like the sort of foreigner any responsible government ought to kill on sight.

But the semantic problems in Iraq run even deeper than that.

For example, there's the "handover of power" that's due to take place on June 30. Since no actual "power" is going to be handed over, the Coalition chaps have had to find a less conclusive phrase. They now talk about the handover of "sovereignty," which is a suitably elastic notion. And, besides, handing over a "notion" is a damn sight easier than handing over anything concrete.

Then again, the U.S. insists that it has been carrying out "negotiations" with the mujahideen in Falluja. These "negotiations" consist of the U.S. military demanding that the mujahideen hand over all their rocket-propelled grenade launchers, in return for which the U.S. military will not blast the city to kingdom come. Now there's a danger that that all sounds like one side "threatening" the other rather than "negotiations"—which, after all, usually imply some give and take on both sides.

As for the word "ceasefire" it's difficult to know what this signifies anymore. According to reliable eyewitness reports from Falluja*, the new American usage makes generous allowance for dropping cluster bombs, flares, and deploying artillery and snipers.

But perhaps the most exciting linguistic development is to be found away from the areas of conflict—in the calm of the Oval Office, where very few people get killed for looking out of their windows. Here, words like "strategy" and "policy" are daily applied to the knee-jerk reactions of politicians and military commanders who think that brute force is the only way to resolve difficult problems in a delicate situation. As Major Kevin Collins, one of the officers in charge of the U.S. Marines in Falluja, put it, "If you choose to pick a fight, we'll finish it."

In the past one might have used a phrase like "numbskull stupidity" rather than "strategy." But then language has a life of its own . . . that is more than one can say for a lot of innocent Iraqis.

*Eyewitness reports by Dahr Jamail and Rahul Mahajan http://newstandardnews.net/dahr.

29.

CONGRATULATIONS TO GEORGE BUSH ON THE GREAT PHOTOS

May 4, 2004

Having seen the photos of American soldiers abusing and humiliating Iraqi prisoners, I would like to congratulate George Bush on finally achieving at least one of his foreign-policy objectives.

I'm afraid that up until now it's been a pretty disappointing record. In fact, the president has failed to achieve almost every single aim in his "War on Terrorism." He has failed to crush Al Qaeda, and he has failed to even find Osama bin Laden. Far from ridding the world of terrorism and bringing peace, he has so enraged Islamic opinion that he has ensured the proliferation of terrorism for the foreseeable future. In Iraq he has failed to find the Weapons of Mass Destruction that were the chief pretext for invading. What's more he has failed to bring democracy, self-government, law and order, and even water and electricity to the people of Iraq.

But now with the photographic evidence of how Iraqis are treated in American jails, President Bush can truthfully claim that some of the unspoken objectives of his "War on Terrorism" are being implemented by the soldiers on the spot.

The dehumanizing of non-Americans, for example, has been a key factor in the administration's policy ever since 9/11. The Patriot Act, which was rushed through on October 26, 2001, guarantees the removal of certain human rights from foreigners on American soil.

The Patriot Act enshrined the right of all noncitizens in the U.S. to be jailed on suspicion and to be detained indefinitely in six-month increments, without proper judicial review and without even having their names published. It's the sort of thing they did in Argentina.

The soldiers at Abu Ghraib prison must, therefore, be given full marks for doing their best—at a local level—to follow through the spirit of the policymakers in Washington.

Contempt for international law has been another mainstay of Mr. Bush's foreign policy for some time now.

In March of last year, Richard Perle, chairman of the defense policy board and a key Bush adviser, spelled out his fervent hope that as well as ending Saddam Hussein's "reign of terror," the invasion of Iraq would also put an end to the major functions of the United Nations. "What will die," (along with Saddam Hussein) he wrote in the *Guardian* (March 21, 2003), "is the fantasy of the UN as the foundation of a new world order," and all that will be left will be "the intellectual wreckage of the liberal conceit of safety through international law administered by international institutions."

Well, the boys at Abu Ghraib couldn't have spelled out their contempt for "international law administered by international institutions" more clearly if they'd been trained to do it!

In particular, they demonstrated their total disregard for the terms of the Geneva Convention, which, of course, is a total wet blanket about things like torture and the humiliation of prisoners.

President Bush attributes the attitude to a handful of soldiers and intelligence officers. But he's being far too modest. These people are only implementing policies that he has had the courage to set in motion.

Guantánamo Bay, was boldly established on non-American soil specifically to avoid the prisoners there claiming access to American law.

And, since Donald Rumsfeld and Co. don't want to be

bothered with all that claptrap about "human rights," which the Geneva Convention so inconveniently applies to prisoners of war, they simply renamed the guys they plucked out of Afghanistan "illegal enemy combatants." Hey, presto! The Geneva Convention no longer applies.

Thus, the jailors in Guantánamo Bay are at liberty to soften up their captives for interrogation with "torture lite"—hooding, isolation, humiliation, general abuse, and so on.

And, in case there is any doubt that this is precisely the way the administration wants the Iraqi prisoners to be treated in Iraq, Mr. Bush has sent Major General Geoffrey Miller to Iraq to sort the problem out. He, of course, is the man who, until now, has been in charge of Guantánamo Bay. Presumably he's been sent to show the jailors in Iraq how to apply the "torture lite" without taking photographs the whole time.

Contempt for non-American human life may not be a stated objective of George Bush's government, but it is implicit in many of their actions—from the assumption that the U.S. has the right to take out any head of state anywhere in the world whom it doesn't like to the refusal to even bother to try and count the Iraqi dead.

Mr. Bush and his colleagues must find it deeply gratifying to see how well ordinary soldiers have imbibed the lessons of their political masters.

WHAT IS IT WITH YOU PEOPLE?? HAVE YOU NEVER SEEN A MAN TAKE A PISS BEFORE?
©Steve Bell 2002

30.

RUMSFELD AND REALITY

May 14, 2004

Donald Rumsfeld reluctantly testified in the investigations into the torture and humiliation of Iraqi prisoners in Abu Ghraib.

I am sure the whole world is grateful to Donald Rumsfeld for pointing out (in his testimony to the Senate Armed Services Committee) that Iraqi detainees are human beings. "I feel terrible about what happened to these Iraqi detainees," he said. "They're human beings."

Many of us, I'm sure, had totally overlooked this important fact. I know there's no real excuse, but, you see, many of us only ever see Iraqi detainees when they've got bags over their heads, and it's very easy for us to forget that people with bags over their heads might be human beings. So I for one am grateful to the defense secretary for reminding us that they are. In fact, I think he should go further.

I think he should also make sure that we realize that the old men, women, and children whom his snipers have been picking off in Falluja are "human beings" as well. The woman hanging up her washing on the roof of her house who was shot by a U.S. sniper, she was human.

The ambulance drivers gunned down while taking the wounded and dying to the hospital—they were human, too . . . so, I imagine, were the wounded and dying. It's so easy to think of them only as "collateral damage" or "insurgents" or "rebels" especially when that's what Mr. Bush and Mr. Blair call them.

Perhaps Mr. Rumsfeld should instruct his people to stress the humanness of these Iraqis when they are announcing the casualty figures in their "War on Terrorism." Except they can't do that, I suppose, because Mr. Rumsfeld has ordered them not to keep count of the Iraqis who get killed while we are still saving them from Saddam Hussein.

It's difficult to see dead Iraqis as human if they don't officially exist.

In fact, Mr. Rumsfeld warns us that this whole "seeing

Iraqis as humans" business is not as easy as one might at first think. Even Mr. Rumsfeld himself has problems, he confides.

In his testimony, the defense secretary revealed that unless he actually sees photos of Iraqis suffering, he has difficulty in conceiving of them as "human beings."

His actual words were: "It is the photographs that gives one the vivid realization of what actually took place. Words don't do it. The words that there were abuses, that it was cruel, that it was inhumane, all of which is true, that it was blatant, you read that and it's one thing. You see the photographs, and you get a sense of it, and you cannot help but be outraged."

You can see his problem. It must be very difficult for him to be in charge of the mightiest military machine on earth when he can only perceive reality through pictures.

I mean, Mr. Rumsfeld might have gone along with the bright idea of putting bags over prisoners heads—even though the European Court of Human Rights declared it to be "a practice of inhuman and degrading treatment"—but, as long as it's just all words, it would never occur to him that it might be a form of torture.

In the same way, the army manual for the treatment of prisoners since 9/11 may recommend hooding and blindfolding, the use of vicious dogs, loud music and bright lights, isolation and forcing detainees into "stress positions" but as long as it's only something in a book, Mr. Rumsfeld is not going to be responsible for what the soldiers on the ground get up to.

And if, by any chance, it turns out that they were doing unpleasant things to their detainees, it's obviously their fault because Mr. Rumsfeld hadn't seen the pictures. He'd only read the reports.

All this may also explain why the defense secretary has been so keen to prevent photos of the coffins of American soldiers appearing in the press or on television. It would never do for the mothers and fathers or even the wider American public to be reminded that these unfortunate young men were once human beings.

No wonder Mr. Rumsfeld has given up looking at newspapers—as he told the U.S. troops in Abu Ghraib—far too many pictures in them.

The actress Cher recently told C-Span broadcasting that she had spent the day at Walter Reed hospital in Washington, D.C. with young American soldiers who had lost arms and legs in Iraq. She said, "I wonder why Cheney, Wolfowitz, Bremer, and the president, aren't having their pictures taken with all these guys?"

I guess it's all part of the same thing: Mr. Rumsfeld's idea that people aren't human unless they've had their photos published. What's more, if Rumsfeld, Cheney, Wolfowitz, Bremer, and the rest saw themselves in photos with the boys their policies have maimed, it might remind them that they too are human, which, judging by the way they wield power, is not how they see themselves.

© Steve Bell 2003
OK NOW LET'S ACCELERATE OUTA THIS SHITHOLE!
STABILITY
DEMOCRACY
PEACE
HUMAN RIGHTS

31.

WHY DOESN'T TONY BLAIR SUPPORT AMERICA?

May 20, 2004

Tony Blair tells us that we should do everything we can to support America. And I agree.

I think we should repudiate those who inflict harm on Americans, we should shun those who bring America itself into disrepute, and we should denounce those who threaten the freedom and democracy that are synonymous with being American.

That is why Tony's recent announcement that he wishes to stand shoulder to shoulder with George Bush is so puzzling.

It's difficult to think of anyone who has inflicted

more harm on Americans than their current president. Well—let me qualify that—it's difficult to think of anyone who has inflicted more harm on *poor* Americans than Mr. Bush.

Since he assumed the title of Most Powerful Man in the World, four million Americans have lost their health insurance and two million jobs have disappeared. According to a CNN report, "Half of all Americans are living from paycheck to paycheck—effectively one paycheck away from poverty."

And Mr. Bush's latest budget proposes to withdraw support of all kinds for working families earning less than $35,000 a year. The House and Senate budget will mean cuts in Medicaid, supplemental health insurance, nutrition assistance, and welfare.

At the same time, the national debt has rocketed to more than $26,000 for every family.

Of course, one should balance all this with Mr. Bush's generosity to the wealthiest 1 percent of Americans, to whom in this year alone he has awarded average tax breaks worth $50,000 per person.

As for bringing America into disrepute, Mr. Bush scores a high rating here, too.

No American president has been so successful in making Americans ashamed of being American. And not just in Baghdad. According to a Gallup Poll last year the majority of Americans—64 percent—"cite a fear of unfriendliness as the top concern of traveling abroad."

And, of course, that was before the photos.

Nowadays, I suppose, the main motive for Americans to travel abroad must be to get away from George Bush's doublespeak.

Of course, during a run-up to an election, all administrations will try to claim credit for spreading largesse even where they don't deserve it, but George Bush's administration has gone one further by trying to claim credit for largesse it has actually been doing its damnedest to stop.

The Justice Department, for example, is boasting about spending forty-seven million dollars on local law enforcement, when Mr. Bush has actually proposed cutting the program by 87 percent.

At the same time, the administration is making election capital out of health care programs that it is really trying to reduce or eliminate altogether. For example, the $11.7 million that the secretary of health and human services boasts they are setting aside to help those without health care, is a program that President Bush has tried to shut down every year he's been in office.

George Bush's doublespeak was also brilliantly employed to persuade Americans to go along with the invasion of Iraq. The president claimed that Saddam had Weapons of Mass Destruction. He didn't. That Saddam had bought uranium yellow cake from Niger to make bombs. He hadn't. That he was linked to Al Qaeda. He wasn't.

It is not often that the State of the Union address has been used as a platform to peddle such a concoction of lies and misconceptions to propagate a war that the president had decided on years before he became president.

President Bush has successfully turned America into a byword for man's inhumanity to man—from torturing its prisoners to massacring over forty people, including fifteen children and ten women at an Iraqi wedding party. The president has left no stone unturned in reversing the good name of Americans throughout the world.

But, perhaps, it is in the area of democracy and freedom that Mr. Bush achieved the most spectacular results.

Mr. Bush's election must represent the nadir of democracy for Americans. And yet Mr. Bush seems perfectly happy to hold onto power even when the majority of Americans didn't vote for him. He says God wants him there. As the undersecretary of defense for intelligence puts it: "George Bush was not elected by a majority of the voters in the U.S. He was appointed by God." I wonder what Sonia Ghandi would have done in George Bush's place?

As for the freedom of which Americans have always been so justly proud, has any president ever done more to undermine it? The American Civil Liberties Union tells us that the Patriot Act that was rushed through Congress in the name of the "War on Terrorism" puts at risk the First, Fourth, Fifth, Sixth, Eighth, and Fourteenth Amendments.

Thousands of men, mostly Arabs or South Asians, have now been secretly imprisoned in America without charge, and the government has refused to publish their names or their whereabouts. They have simply been "disappeared." Don't cry for me, Argentina.

What is more, religious and political organizations can now be freely spied on by the government without evidence of wrongdoing. Non-Americans can be tried in secret and convicted on hearsay, while even Americans can now be held in military custody without charges and without access to lawyers.

And to top it all off, Mr. Bush's attorney general has just fished out an old 1872 law (last used in 1890), designed to stop prostitutes way-laying sailors, to prevent Greenpeace exercising its right to peaceful protest.

In the same week, we learned that the mighty Disney company is afraid of releasing Michael Moore's latest film because it might endanger the tax breaks on its theme park and hotels in Florida, where the president's brother, Jeb, is governor. So much for free speech.

In fact the more I think about it, America hardly seems like America anymore.

If Tony Blair really were concerned about helping Americans he would surely be helping them to reclaim their country and institutions from this catastrophic presidency. The one thing he would not be doing would be standing "shoulder to shoulder" with George Bush.

32.

IT REALLY ISN'T TORTURE

June 14, 2004

For some time now I've been trying to find out where my son goes after choir practice. He simply refuses to tell me. He says it's no business of mine where he goes after choir practice and it's a free country.

Now, it may be a free country, but if people start going just anywhere they like after choir practice goodness knows whether we'll have a country left to be free. I mean he might be going to anarchist meetings or Islamic study groups. How do I know?

The thing is if people don't say where they're going after choir practice, this country is at risk. So, I have been applying a certain amount of pressure on my son to tell me where he's going.

To begin with I simply put a bag over his head and chained him to a radiator. But did that persuade him? Does the Pope eat kosher?

My wife had the gall to suggest that I might be going a bit too far. So I put a bag over her head and chained her to the radiator.

But I still couldn't persuade my son to tell me where he goes after choir practice.

I tried starving him, serving him only cold meals, and shaving off his facial hair, keeping him in stress positions, not turning his light off, playing loud music outside his cell door—all the usual stuff that any concerned parent will do to find out where their child is going after choir practice. But it was all to no avail.

I hesitated to gravitate to harsher interrogation methods because, after all he is my son. Then Donald Rumsfeld came to my rescue.

I read in the *New York Times* last week that a memo had been prepared for the defense secretary on March 6, 2003. It laid down the strictest guidelines as to what is and what is not torture. Because, let's face it, none of us want to actually torture our children in case the police get to hear about it.

The March 6 memo prepared for Mr. Rumsfeld

explained what may look like torture is not really torture at all. It states that if someone "knows that severe pain will result from his actions, if causing such harm is not his objective, he lacks the requisite specific intent even though the defendant did not act in good faith."

What this means, in understandable English, is that if a parent, in his anxiety to know where his son goes after choir practice, does something that will cause severe pain to his son, it is only "torture" if the causing of that severe pain is his objective. If his objective is something else—such as finding out where his son goes after choir practice—then it is not torture.

Mr. Rumsfeld's memo goes on: "A defendant" (by which he means a concerned parent) "is guilty of torture only if he acts with the express purpose of inflicting severe pain or suffering on a person within his control."

Couldn't be clearer. If your intention is to extract information, you cannot be accused of torture.

In fact, the report went further. It said, if a parent "has a good faith belief his actions will not result in prolonged mental harm, he lacks the mental state necessary for his actions to constitute torture." So, all you've got to do, to avoid accusations of child abuse, is to say that you didn't think it would cause any lasting harm to the child. Easy peasy!

I have currently got a lot of my son's friends locked up

in the garage, and I'm applying electrical charges to their genitals and sexually humiliating them in order to get them to tell me where my son goes after choir practice.

Dick Cheney's counsel, David S. Addington, says that's just fine. William J. Haynes, the Defense Department's general counsel, agrees it's just fine. And so does the air force general counsel, Mary Walker.

In fact, practically everybody in the U.S. administration seems to think it's just fine, except for the State Department lawyer, William H. Taft IV, who perversely claims that I might be opening the door to people applying electrical charges to *my* genitals and sexually humiliating *me*.

So, I'm going to round up all the children in the neighborhood, chain them up, and set dogs on them, I might accidentally kill one or two—but I won't have intended to—and perhaps I'll take some photos of my wife standing on the dead bodies and then I'll show the photos to the other kids and, finally—perhaps—I might get to find out where my son goes after choir practice.

After all, I'll only be doing what the present U.S. administration has been condoning since 9/11.

QUIET PROGRESS:
CONDITIONS ARE IMPROVING INSIDE IRAQ. DO YOU:
(a) AGREE STRONGLY
(b) AGREE
(c) HAVE NO OPINION
(d) DISAGREE
(e) DISAGREE STRONGLY
(f) CANNOT SAY BECAUSE YOU ARE DEAD OR OTHERWISE INDISPOSED
SHOCK
AWE

33.

IN IRAQ, IT'S ALREADY JULY NINTH

July 7, 2004

As we mark the first full week of Iraqi sovereignty, the world is only just beginning to appreciate the full significance of the historic handover ceremony, which was hurried through in secret two days before it was due and without any of the top people present.

It is now clear that this may well be a blueprint for all future state occasions and festivities in this age of terrorism. President Bush is expected to order that, from now on, July 4 should be celebrated at least two days earlier, although the White House will reserve the right to declare July 4 in June or even May, if need be. The president also will have full powers to announce that Thanksgiving has been and gone before any terrorist has had a chance to mark the occasion with violence.

Furthermore, all public ceremonies will be held in private and will last no more than twenty minutes. Any American official involved should be given the chance to get safely away before an announcement is made, when events may be restaged for the television cameras.

But perhaps the most important lesson to be learnt from the handover of sovereignty ceremony in Iraq is that on no account should any ceremony actually mean anything.

Condoleezza Rice wrote to President Bush that "Iraq is sovereign," which, according to my dictionary, means "independent of outside authority." The reality, of course, is that Iraq has 140,000 American troops stationed on its soil, whom the Iraqi government cannot get rid of and over whom it has no control, other than authorizing more bombings in Falluja. Nor can the new sovereign government prosecute any Americans or other foreigners who have killed, maimed, or tortured Iraqi civilians over the past year.

Before he hurried off, Paul Bremer thoughtfully wrote most of the new government's laws for it, including capping all income and corporate taxes at 15 percent and banning Iraqis from driving with only one hand on the steering wheel. And he's framed his laws in a way that the new sovereign government of Iraq can do nothing whatsoever about.

It goes without saying that it can't rescind Order 39, which throws Iraq open for foreign investment far beyond World Bank guidelines or what is practiced by Britain and the U.S. Foreign companies are now free to plunder the Iraqi economy to their hearts' content, without having to reinvest locally or guarantee that at least some revenues go back to the Iraqis. And the sovereign government of Iraq can whistle if it doesn't like it.

The handover of "sovereignty" was just as meaningless as the handover of Saddam Hussein from U.S. to Iraqi control. He's still held by the Americans in a secret location, but "legally" he's now in "Iraqi control." It's just something you say, not something you actually mean.

Secrecy and control must become our watchwords if democracy is to survive in the age of terrorism and continue to confront the enemies of freedom—tyrants, such as Saddam Hussein, who operate by secrecy and control that are the very opposite of our own traditions.

BREMER - I WANT AN EXIT STRATEGY OR YOU'RE ON YOUR WAY OUT!!

PRESIDENT'S SECOND SURPRISE VISIT:
IT'LL ALL BE OVER BY CHRISTMAS, GUYS!
ARMY

Acknowledgments

I would like to thank Seamus Milne at *The Guardian*, Mike Holland at *The Observer* and Simon O'Hagan at *The Independent* for encouraging me to write these pieces, and I would like to thank those newspapers for permission to reprint them. I would also like to thank Anna Kiernan for persuading me to contribute to *Voices For Peace* and Simon & Schuster for permission to reprint. Thanks also to Helen Akif for suggesting I make a collection and to my wife Alison Telfer for helping to collect them and to Carl Bromley for putting it all together and making it possible.